BACK TO MANHATTAN

A LIFE IN NEW YORK

David Garnes

Indian Pipe Publishing

2019

Dedication

To my friends from the New York years
...some gone, all remembered

Special mention to Elaine Congress,
lifelong friend

Table of Contents

Acknowledgments...v

Foreword ix

Dallas and New York: November 1963 1

Belgian Waffles and the Virgin Mary................................9

The Majestic Heart of a Campus 16

Taylor and Burton: With Liz 'n Dick in Times Square.....22

Where I Was When the Lights Went Out..........................27

Nickel Afternoons on the Staten Island Ferry..................34

Alone in the Dark..38

Up against the Wall! Part I: Columbia 1968 45

A Pigeon Cooed in Gramercy Park 57

My Days and Nights at the Plaza....................................63

The Other Cathedral in Manhattan 72

Hot Town..79

Vanished in Manhattan..88

Bus Ride to the Middle Ages 94

1001 Nights at The New York City Ballet 98

Up against the Wall! Part II: Stonewall 1969 105

Random Thoughts of a Depressed New Yorker.............114

Always an Onlooker, Never an Extra 120

Nights in Sheridan Square 129

Behind the Curtain: The Professional
Children's School.. 135

A Walk on the Wild Side.. 142

Falafels, Egg Creams, and Breakfast at Tom's 151

Credits 161

Photo Credits... 162

Acknowledgments

Thanks to the members of my writing group—Christine Andersen, Lynn Chirico, Marsha Howland, Sarah Karstaedt, and Nancy Walker—for their encouragement, insightful criticism, and friendship.

Special thanks to Mary Heaney, enthusiastic reader, astute editor, wise friend.

And a tip of the cap to the phenomenon that is New York, the best city in the world to discover, experience, relish, and remember what life has to offer.

One can't paint New York as it is,
but rather as it is felt.

Georgia O'Keeffe

Foreword

When I moved to the Upper West Side of Manhattan as a Columbia grad student, JFK was president and Times Square teemed with porn. Robert F. Wagner, Jr. was serving his third term as mayor, having survived the departure of the Dodgers and Giants by bringing in a new baseball franchise, the New York Metropolitans. Entrapment of gay men by New York's finest was in high gear.

By the time I departed for Connecticut in the early 1980s, the city was approaching the tail end of a decline that had made daily life a challenge. There were more robberies in 1981 than at any time in the city's history. When I took the subway home late at night, I always walked down the center of my side street, skirting the shadows of brownstone steps and recessed basement entrances. Ed Koch, who had become mayor in 1977 on a "law and order" platform, had just begun his second term, elected with a 75 percent majority. Times Square was still a hotbed of sleaze.

On the other hand, by 1981 the gay rights movement was well established. Over at Lincoln Center, just a big hole in the ground when I moved to the city in '63, the New York City Ballet was packing them in. The word "Internet" was being heard more frequently, and online catalogs had begun to replace the hundreds of little oak drawers I perused regularly in my work in Columbia's Butler Library.

I came of age in New York and for 18 years took full advantage of what the city had to offer. As Hemingway wrote of 1920s Paris, "A great city has a way of making a lasting impression." I was young and curious and eager to be as much a part of the banquet as any hungry guest, and New York's moveable feast sustains me still.

Life changes, however, and one moves with the current of circumstance and the challenge of choice. And so I left New York for the suburbs of Eastern Connecticut. I'd been fortunate, for years, to be part of the unsurpassed wealth of culture the city offered—the bookstores, art house movie theaters, the virtually free summer concerts. When I witnessed the student uprising at Columbia and participated in Stonewall and the early days of gay liberation, I felt I was at the very center of the enormous societal changes that characterized the second half of the American century.

Do I regret leaving the city? Mostly, no. Though living in New York still provided excitement and new adventures, by the early 80s it had become as much a burden—hectic and stressful—as an ongoing adventure. I was ready to leave.

Do I miss being in Manhattan? Often. I miss the theater, the museums, the night life, the friends I left behind, though many of them, like me, have moved away. Others have died.

Do I still consider myself a New Yorker? Yes, for sure. When I said goodbye at 40, I knew it would always be part of who I am. The city formed me, and I can't imagine my life without the years I spent there.

Here is what I remember.

Dallas and New York:
November 1963

At precisely 1:36 pm, November 22, 1963 on an ABC radio affiliate in New York City, Doris Day's rendition of the upbeat song "Hooray for Hollywood" was abruptly cut off by the following statement:

"We interrupt this program to bring you a special bulletin. Three shots were fired at President Kennedy's motorcade today in downtown Dallas, Texas…We're going to stand by for more details on the incident…Now we return you to your regular programming."

I was sitting at my desk in the busy Midtown office of Allied International, an aeronautics export company on Park Avenue. I was stuck in the middle of a bothersome sentence in French that I was having trouble turning into business English, and I was tired and bored. Usually I only half-listened to the background music and disc-jockey chatter that was piped into my workspace. However, I was—and am—a great fan of Doris Day, so I was immediately aware of what had just been said.

The announcement was short and inconclusive enough that I'd hardly had time to react when Doris was cut off again—this time permanently—as the announcer continued to give additional details of the shooting. *"The President was seen slumped over in the car...President Kennedy and Texas Governor John Connally, also wounded, have been rushed to nearby Parkland Hospital...The President has been given the last rites of the Catholic Church."*

Within an hour we learned that JFK was dead.

After initial gasps, exclamations, and teary gatherings around our desks, we staff all returned to our work stations to continue listening to more bulletins and, I suppose, to attempt to get back to our respective duties, irrelevant and unimportant as they'd suddenly become.

My first thought was to call my roommate Charlie, who I knew would be home studying. We were both first-year grad students at Columbia on the Upper West Side of Manhattan. I worked several hours a week at Allied as a translator of correspondence—French to English for incoming letters, English to French for replies.

As I suspected, Charlie had not been listening to the radio. I recall telling him the news with that particular sense of drama you feel when you know you're the first messenger of a startling piece of information. Charlie at first thought I was kidding, but it was impossible for me to continue without my voice breaking. Charlie, a political science major and fervent admirer of Kennedy, was stunned into silence, and we cut our conversation short.

I realized I'd been shaken, profoundly. I too had been an ardent Kennedy supporter since his tenure as senator from my home state of Massachusetts. In the presidential campaign, I loved watching his debates with Nixon, the first ever to be televised. In the initial debate, Nixon came across like a pale, semi-sinister henchman with a five o'clock shadow—a character from a bad B movie—very much in contrast to the ebullience and charisma of the handsome Jack Kennedy.

Another memory of JFK involved the Cuban missile crisis of October 1962. I was a senior in college on the night he gave the speech announcing an embargo on any military materiel being shipped to Cuba. After his talk, my friends and I contemplated the great likelihood that before the year was over, we'd be pulled out of school and drafted into an all-out war. But Khrushchev backed down, compromise was reached, and the President recouped a great deal of the diplomatic cachet lost in the disastrous and embarrassing Bay of Pigs invasion 18 months earlier.

As these thoughts raced through my mind, Mr. and Mrs. Ulmann, the owners of the export company, came out of their offices and told us that we could all go home; the place was closing early. Alec Ulmann, an impeccably dressed Russian-born engineer, and Mary, his formidable English wife, also ran the prestigious 12 Hours of Sebring in Florida, modeled after the Grand Prix races on the continent. They had contacts in Europe, and occasionally I'd work on interesting letters involving that business. I knew from previous conversations we'd had that they were staunch Republicans, but I could tell that the assassination had stunned even the usually imperturbable Mary Ulmann.

I said goodbye to my colleagues and took the elevator down to the marble, bronze, and chandelier-lit lobby of the

New York Central Building (now the Helmsley). I walked next door, through the gigantic Pan Am tower (since renamed the MetLife) with its then-heliport roof, and proceeded down the escalator into Grand Central Terminal. The vast rotunda was, as usual, teeming, but except for the muffled echoes of thousands of feet on the marble floor, the place was eerily silent. No one seemed to be talking.

I exited Grand Central on Vanderbilt, a short avenue running a few blocks north and south between Park and Madison. I was restless, so I decided to stop at my downstairs Horn & Hardart Automat across the narrow, skyscraper-shadowed street. The cashier in the elevated cage in the center of the restaurant was changing bills and larger coins for nickels, but I still had a handful left over from my lunch there earlier in the day (one of my favorites, their famous baked beans served in an oblong dish with a hot dog neatly nestled on top).

Filling a cup with coffee from one of the fancy gold spigots, I put a few nickels into a little glass-slotted box that held a saucer of rice pudding, and then I sat at one of the few unoccupied tables. You could easily tell by watching the expressions and conversations of the customers which of them already knew what had happened in Dallas, as opposed to those who were just hearing the news from other customers.

It was a mild afternoon for November and I was still edgy after my snack, so instead of taking the underground shuttle over to the West Side IRT subway, I walked across 42nd Street, past the big windows of Stern's Department Store, and across the street, the New York Public Library and Bryant Park. As I approached the decidedly sleazier environs of Times Square past Fifth Avenue, the streets were crowded and the traffic noisy, but, again, most of the pedestrians were silent.

I avoided what I imagined was the mob already gathered beneath the revolving news ticker at One Times Square and instead boarded the IRT local further north at 50th Street. Here, the effect on the crowd of JFK's sudden death was most apparent. No stampeding out and in of arriving trains, no shoving, and virtually no conversation as the cars lumbered through the dark tunnels to the upper West Side. I have never, before or since, had that experience in a Manhattan subway. We were like dazed extras from *Invasion of the Body Snatchers.*

After I got to my apartment on West 101st Street, my roommate and I stayed rooted to our small-screen portable TV with its giant rabbit ears for virtually the entire weekend. My recollection is that except for a quick trip to the Columbia library and bathroom visits and occasional deli runs, Charlie and I watched Walter Cronkite (then the trusted "daddy" of American journalists) for hours and hours. It seemed like Cronkite was on camera for the duration, but I also do recall a young Dan Rather, who, after nabbing two priests at Parkland Hospital, had been the first commentator to break the unofficial, but sadly accurate, news of the President's death.

In the nearly 50 years that have passed since that weekend, so much of what we watched and experienced has been rebroadcast and rehashed that it's hard to distinguish between what you really remember first-hand and what you learned later. Like a family story that's been passed down for generations or a classic movie you never saw but have come to think you did, memory and external knowledge intermingle. The magnitude of the killing, the sheer shock of the president's death, the underlying uncertainty of what was to come, also contributed to the sense that we were, indeed, watching a melodrama with more than its share of improbable twists and turns.

The killing of Dallas police officer J. D. Tippet, presumably by Lee Harvey Oswald, and Oswald's capture shortly thereafter at the Texas, a rundown dollar movie theater, came next in a series of rapidly unfolding events. In the meantime, we'd also seen photos of Vice-President Lyndon B. Johnson taking the presidential oath of office, a sad Lady Bird Johnson and Jackie Kennedy, her face an expressionless mask, standing on either side of him. Much was made of the fact that Mrs. Kennedy continued to wear the blood-stained pink suit she'd had on in the motorcade, but, as we later learned, much more of the blood and brains of the President had been removed from her face, hair, and clothes by then.

Perhaps the most bizarre development was the freakish murder, captured on live television, of the purported assassin by one Jack Ruby, owner of a strip joint in Dallas. What we witnessed on the small screen—Oswald's grimace, Ruby being wrestled to the floor, a detective in a white cowboy hat shouting, "Jack, you son of a bitch!"—didn't seem like it could possibly have happened. But it had, and as the omnipresent Walter Cronkite used to say on another show, "You were there."

On Sunday Charlie and I watched the solemn procession to the Capitol, to the sound of drums, and the subsequent lying in state of JFK's casket. Live coverage of the events in Washington were supplemented on all three networks— NBC, CBS, and ABC—by endless conversations, reports, and reminiscences with people ranging from bystanders near the infamous grassy knoll to schoolchildren in Ireland to television anchor Chet Huntley, the NBC commentator we occasionally switched the channel to hear.

Images of the funeral that we watched live on Monday, only three days after the assassination, have become iconic photographs: three-year-old John Kennedy Jr. saluting as his father's casket passed; French President Charles de Gaulle towering over Emperor Haile Selassie of Ethiopia at Arlington Cemetery; Mrs. Kennedy in her black dress, hat, and veil walking between her brothers-in-law, Bobby and Ted, to the graveside. Ironically, President Kennedy had been at Arlington exactly two weeks earlier to pay homage at the Tomb of the Unknown Soldier.

And then it was over, and the next day, Tuesday, November 26, we returned to the busyness of our daily lives. Thanksgiving was coming up, and I went home to spend the holiday weekend with my family in New England. Semester exams followed, and then I was busy writing my thesis on the poetry of Emily Dickinson.

JFK was gone, and the world did not end. But along with his assassination also died a certain belief in the possibilities of a new age of...what...something different, at any rate, from the status quo and complacency of the Eisenhower years.

The first mention of "Camelot" appeared in a Life magazine interview between political writer Theodore H. White and Jacqueline Kennedy shortly after November 22. During their talk, the former first lady adroitly spoke of her husband's administration as the dawn of a "period of hope and optimism, like King Arthur's kingdom." This analogy, perhaps a bit calculated but somehow apt, stuck.

What Kennedy's presidency might have accomplished had he served a second term we'll never know. But other big changes were about to happen. What followed before the decade was over—Vietnam, the civil rights movement, women's lib, and the beginning of gay liberation—altered forever the fabric of American life as we college kids of the early 60s—the Kennedy years—knew it.

Belgian Waffles
and the Virgin Mary

Waffle…Belgian…Belgian Waffle: Does this name conjure up a sweet trip down memory lane? If so, chances are you're one of the multitudes who helped make this sinfully delectable treat the culinary sensation of the 1964-1965 New York World's Fair.

Consisting of an ordinary waffle topped with a generous dollop of strawberries and whipped cream, the Belgian Waffle ruled. It was originally sold only at the elaborate four-acre recreation of a medieval village at the Belgium pavilion, but soon the BW became a fair-wide concession staple. The Unisphere, Swiss Sky Ride, and Michelangelo's *Pietà* notwithstanding, that waffle is probably what visitors remember best. A close second is probably the "It's a Small World" Pepsi exhibit and that earworm song, warbled in a United Nations of languages by animated dolls.

I'd been in New York about a year when the fair opened. Over the course of its first season and well into its second summer, I hosted out-of-town family and friends many times on treks out to the fairgrounds, just a subway ride away in

Queens. Counting visits on my own, I was 'way up in the double digits by the time the gates closed forever in the fall of '65.

I was familiar with the celebrated 1939 New York World's Fair from many small, scalloped-edged snapshots my mother had saved, but the 1964 fair was the first of this magnitude that most of us on the Eastern seaboard had experienced. Though figures in red on the fair's fiscal ledgers apparently record heavy losses—unlike the profitable Seattle Fair two years earlier—I don't think I knew anyone at the time who hadn't paid a visit and dropped some cash, and I don't mean just on a waffle and a Pepsi. There were several expensive restaurants, most notably the Toledo at the Spain pavilion, as well as pricey, imported items for sale at many of the other foreign exhibits.

A major theme of the fair involved a look into the future, and some of the giants of American industry—Ford, GE, Westinghouse—were represented by elaborate displays of what we could all look forward to as the century progressed: visual telephoning, sophisticated robots, space travel. The intention was to create a sense of optimism and well-being. I oohed and aahed along with everyone else at the prospect of what was to come.

This focus on the future was also evident in the striking architecture of the enormous egg-shaped IBM building, designed by famed architect Eero Saarinen, and the spectacular Futurama moving car ride at the General Motors pavilion, where we rode past images of moon voyages we were told might happen in our lifetime.

It was no accident that the master of magical images, Walt Disney, collaborated on several exhibits and rides. In addition to the Pepsi exhibit, these included GE's "Carousel of Progress," a revolving, animated panorama of the history of electricity; "Magic Skyway," where we traveled on brand-new Ford cars through elaborate prehistoric and futuristic creations; and, of course, those frolicking, ceaselessly trilling children and animals in the "It's a Small World" show.

I remember the colors of the fair as bold, the buildings and vehicles gleaming against the sky. The four-passenger cars of the Swiss Sky Ride, seemingly everywhere, were cartoon-bright red and yellow and green and blue. The New York Pavilion, a Philip Johnson creation, consisted of a series of circular towers supporting a mammoth canopy, the "Tent of Tomorrow," in shades of bright orange and turquoise. Just outside the fairgrounds, the original Shea Stadium, which opened five days before the fair, mirrored this same color scheme on its exterior walls.

Even the subway that transported millions of us from Times Square to Queens was new, a fleet of 400 trains painted aqua and white. Though graffiti-spattered cars hadn't yet become the norm (that was to happen a decade later), these trains were vastly different from your run-of-the-mill Broadway local. Granted, they weren't air-conditioned (no cars in the system were then), but the fans worked better and the interiors were clean. By the time the sleek trains arrived at the fairgrounds, we were primed for the spanking new exhibits spread over the sprawling square mile of Flushing Meadows.

The symbolic center of the fair and the place most visitors seemed to be drawn to was the Unisphere. A stainless steel, 12-story model of the Earth, it was surrounded by fountains spouting white water high into the sky. I'd guess there are more Kodacolor prints of the Unisphere fading away in forgotten basement and attic scrapbooks than of any other structure. I have a late-day shot of my mother and aunt posing front and center of the globe, game smiles for the camera belying their aching feet. In addition to those ubiquitous Swiss sky cars, there was some ground transportation available, but seeing the sights involved lots and lots of walking.

One of the most popular attractions at the fair, right up there with the spookily lifelike Abraham Lincoln robot at the Illinois Pavilion (Disney again), was the celebrated *Pietà* of Michelangelo. Transported carefully, very carefully, across the Atlantic from St. Peter's Basilica in Rome, this sculpted masterpiece was anchored in elaborate casing on the Italian Line's Cristoforo Columbo. Ironically, this liner was the sister ship of the Andrea Doria, which had sunk a few years earlier off Nantucket Island, also en route to New York.

Safely ensconced in the fair's Vatican Pavilion in an overly air-conditioned gallery, the *Pietà* became one of the fair's most celebrated sights. On my very first visit to the fairgrounds, I waited in line for an hour before being directed to one of four multilevel conveyor platforms. As we slowly glided sideways to the sonorous, piped-in sounds of a Gregorian chant, the life-sized sculpture came into view: a sorrowful but composed Mary cradling her crucified son. Strategically situated under a halo of flickering lights in an otherwise darkened room, the *Pietà* sat behind a huge Plexiglas screen against a background of dark blue.

Aside from the mobile conveyor, was I otherwise moved by this encounter with one of the great objects of Western art? Yes and no. The serene beauty of the faces of Mary and Jesus made an indelible impression. On the other hand, the chilliness of the chamber, as well as the focused light that cast a whitish hue on the statue, diminished for me what should have been an emotional experience commensurate with the poignancy of the image. I could have also done without the music and the sensation of being on a horizontal escalator.

A few years after its safe return to the Vatican, the *Pietà* was severely damaged by a deranged viewer who claimed to be both Jesus Christ and Michelangelo. During a visit to Italy in 1977, I saw the restored *Pietà* again, this time up close. I was struck by the richness and intricacy of the sculpture— the seamless folds in Mary's robes, for example—and the somewhat darker, warmer shades of the Carrrara marble, effects that had been flattened, possibly distorted, by the austere lighting in New York. And I was able to take it all in at my own pace. The *Pietà* is a work to be admired in peaceful reflection.

From another high-class display of originals by Velazquez, Goya, El Greco, and Picasso at the Spanish Pavilion to Bourbon Street's "Les Poupées de Paris," a risqué review featuring topless puppets, the fair was nothing if not eclectic in its offerings. By the time it ended in September1965, I'd become somewhat of an expert on what to see on a marathon one-day visit.

During that second summer, I occasionally searched out new places while my friends were standing in line to hear Abraham Lincoln's resonant words of wisdom or waiting to be serenaded over in Pepsiland by "Dünya küçük!," Turkish for "It's a Small World." One afternoon, in an impulsive moment, I entered a small, unimpressive building, paid a dollar, and descended into a fascinating exhibit called "The Underground World Home."

Situated entirely beneath the surface of swampy meadowland, this well-appointed house, built inside a 5600-square-foot concrete shell, had three bedrooms, a garden with real flowers, and a spacious terrace. Panoramic photographs on the "windows" created a surprisingly credible illusion of the outdoors, with automatic timers controlling daytime and evening views.

As a kid, I'd experienced "duck and cover" air raid drills in school and the brief craze for bomb shelters during the Cold War, so this was not a concept totally foreign to my 1950s psyche. Too, I'd always been fascinated by subterranean life, be it Alice's rabbit hole, the cozy North Pole headquarters of Father Christmas that Babar the elephant fell into, or the wonders of Jules Verne's *Journey to the Center of the Earth*, which I'd read as a Classics Illustrated comic book.

I didn't pay much attention to the construction stats our enthusiastic guide rattled off, but I was intrigued by the concept of a hidden world, or at least a secret getaway. The Underground World Home was right up my alley.

Though a real-estate boom in below-ground dwellings did not evolve in subsequent decades, less than four years after the fair ended we did land on the moon, certainly "a giant step for mankind" and a fulfillment of what was predicted in the Hall of Science's space exhibit.

In addition to providing a glimpse into the future, another theme of the '64-'65 fair, heavily touted, was "Peace Through Understanding," a concept that had already been sorely tested several times since the end of World War II, only 19 years earlier. The escalating conflict in Vietnam (200,000 deployed American troops by 1965) only adds in retrospect to the painful irony of this slogan.

Recently, I watched a "YouTube" video clip from the original "It's a Small World" show. Though I began by humming along, I confess that most of the lyrics came back to me. Simplistic and somewhat monotonous, the song also struck me, surprisingly, as honest and real.. "There's so much that we share/That it's time we're aware/It's a small world after all."

Fifty-plus years later, with the planet virtually smaller but political and social schisms ever greater, these last lines are now a poignant reminder to me of the "they-all-lived-happily-ever-after" future the fair so cheerfully, confidently, and ingenuously promised.

The Majestic Heart of a Campus

Entering through the massive iron gates at 116th Street and Broadway and standing in the center of the Columbia University campus for the first time remains an indelible memory: the sweeping steps, huge columns, and Pantheon-like dome of Low Library rising to the north, the equally imposing colonnade and multi-storied windows of Butler Library at the end of the wide walkway on my right.

These two massive structures and virtually all the others within sight, many of them creations of the legendary McKim, Mead, and White architectural firm, were of a scale and grandeur I hadn't encountered before.

I was more than impressed, and I've never forgotten that moment. Indeed, the vast quadrangle was—and remained for many years—the focal point of my academic and professional life.

I arrived at Columbia as a graduate student in the fall of 1963. Though I'd visited New York a number of times, I hadn't really experienced living in a big city and certainly not life on a sprawling urban campus. I was eager, and I was ready.

I'd just spent four years as an undergraduate at Brown University, situated on the crest of a steep hill overlooking a then somewhat tired and dilapidated New England city, certainly not the Providence that has revived itself, phoenix-like, in recent years. The Brown campus itself—crisscrossed by narrow, tree-lined streets dating from Colonial times—was lovely, but it might have been situated on the periphery of any quasi-urban American city struggling to stay afloat midst the post-war migration to the suburbs. Its location on the hill almost seemed like a defiant and deliberate separation from the realities of the decaying downtown below. It was in, but not of, mid-20th century Providence.

Columbia, on the other hand, was in 1963 not only in the center of a huge metropolis but also surrounded on all sides by similarly deteriorating, yet incredibly vibrant, neighborhoods—a once comfortable Upper West Side Jewish enclave on its west and south, and miles of the mean streets of Harlem and Spanish Harlem to the east and north. Granted, the slope on the eastern edge of Morningside Heights and the adjoining Morningside Park served as a convenient barrier of sorts to these Black and Hispanic ghettos.

Neighborhood issues would in fact become the catalyst in the late 1960s for the student uprisings that grew to symbolize much of the discontent of that era and which are described elsewhere in this book. But even in my early days on campus, I never felt isolated from the real world at Columbia as I had at Brown.

Emerging from the subway after a quick ride up from, say, Midtown Times Square on the IRT local, I had only a few steps to walk before entering the enormous quad. Though there was a startling contrast between what was outside the gates and what was within, I never forgot where I was: balanced on the northern reaches of an island that encompassed, within a given block or two, both enormous privilege and abject poverty.

During my years at Columbia, I grew increasingly familiar with most of the campus buildings surrounding the quad. St. Paul's Chapel, for example, is a Renaissance Revival gem with a sumptuous Byzantine interior, once called "the best of all Columbia's buildings" by the American Institute of Architects.

When I worked at Butler Library, I occasionally meandered across the quad at lunchtime to spend a few quiet moments in St. Paul's. Sitting in one of the movable chairs, I'd follow the hazy light filtering down from the dome and illuminating the stained glass windows behind the altar. The windows depict St. Paul preaching in front of the Parthenon, a fitting allusion to the University's designation as the "Acropolis of Morningside Heights."

Buell Hall, a small gabled structure next door to St. Paul's, served for many years as the offices of the School of General Studies, founded in the post-World War II era for returning veterans attending college under the GI Bill. It now houses the Maison Française. This charming building, the oldest on campus and all that remains of the Bloomingdale Insane Asylum, was constructed specifically to accommodate wealthy male patients. Situated amid the hinterland farms of upper Manhattan in the early nineteenth century, the asylum was reached by the only road on the island extending that far to the north, now called Broadway.

Today, strolling from one elegant academic building to another on brick paths bordered by manicured shrubs and carefully tended flower beds, it's hard to imagine this earlier, natural bucolic setting, testimony to the rapid growth of the island and a startling reminder of the presence of the university back in the days preceding urban sprawl. The intention of the trustees to establish Columbia big-time on the then sparsely populated upper reaches of Manhattan was made clear by the hiring of McKim, Mead, and White to design the new campus. The Brooklyn Museum, the magnificent Pennsylvania Station and its adjoining architectural counterpart, the huge Farley Post Office, were all creations of this firm.

Sanford White, one of the founding partners of McKim, Mead, and White, and the principal designer of the Washington Square Arch, achieved greater notoriety when he was shot by the husband of his young lover, the notorious Evelyn Nesbit, also known as "the girl in the red velvet swing." This murder, quickly dubbed "the crime of the century," took place on a balmy June night a few miles south of Morningside Heights in the roof garden theater of the second Madison Square Garden, another White design. The actual shooting happened during the show's finale, aptly titled "I Could Love a Million Girls."

Earl Hall, another, smaller McKim, Mead, and White building on the opposite side of Low and long the venue for student religious activities, became notable in the early 1970s for the gay dances ("open to all") that were held on Friday nights in its basement. I'd ended my student days several years earlier and never attended, but it was heartening to see Columbia in the forefront of the liberation movement that took hold after the Stonewall uprising down in Greenwich Village in 1969.

I was recently reminded of another historical fact while I was doing research for a novel that is partially set in the Columbia neighborhood of the post-World War II decade. Until that time, the main quad was actually bisected by 116th Street. In 1953, under Dwight D. Eisenhower's brief Columbia presidency, the street was blocked off. Nothing remains now that would indicate that cars, taxis, and buses once traversed the space between the two gates bordering, respectively, Broadway and Amsterdam Avenue. A deliberate move toward academic isolationism? Perhaps, though the open area now provides a safe and spacious pedestrian landscape for students and neighborhood residents alike.

If I did have any initial ideas when I first arrived at Columbia about the inviolate character of the campus as it related—or not—to the surrounding neighborhood, that sense of ivory tower serenity and security was blown away by the student demonstrations that tore the campus apart, literally and figuratively, in 1968.

Even now, years later, on occasional visits to the Upper West Side, when I see students reclining in the sun on the wide sloping steps of Low Library, I think of less tranquil times. I remember friends who witnessed police forcibly evicting protesters from occupied buildings and into paddy wagons, their beaten bodies bruised, heads bumping on the steps as they were dragged past the statue of Alma Mater, herself covered with graffiti proclaiming—for the most part, truthfully—the administration's seeming indifference to brutality and its tacit support of the senseless and futile Vietnam War.

From that time on, the campus, and the quad in particular, became for me a complicated, dynamic symbol of the co-existence of societal inequalities and ills with extraordinary architectural creativity and academic achievement. As many times as I made my way across this expanse—I was later a librarian in Butler for many years—I was always aware of being in a singular, perhaps unique, place.

Is there any other New York landmark so physically and historically bound to the dense urban space that surrounds it? Is there any other campus whose architectural heart is so majestic and thrilling?

Taylor and Burton:
With Liz 'n Dick in Times Square

The recent death of Elizabeth Taylor has got me to thinking about the nature of celebrity.

We both worship and revile our larger-than-life icons, and their fame can teeter between untouchable idolatry to scornful judgment. Though revered in later years for her good deeds, Taylor was the target of a slew of slings and arrows half a century ago. At the height of the Roman scandal involving Richard Burton during the filming of *Cleopatra*, a member of Congress wanted Taylor and her paramour barred from the USA on the grounds of "undesirability," and the official Vatican newspaper condemned her as a "woman of loose morals" who exemplified "erotic vagrancy."

My own memory of Liz is somewhat different.

It was a warm night in Midtown Manhattan in the spring of 1964. As I and several hundred other playgoers shuffled out of the Lunt-Fontanne Theater on West 46th Street, we were greeted by stalled traffic, beeping horns, tobacco smoke and exhaust fumes, all part of the usual late evening theater scene. But the presence of mounted police and several cop cars double-parked next to waiting limousines was not. Something else was up.

"Is it usually like this these days?" I asked one of New York's finest, sitting astride a big, majestic chestnut.

"Every night," he replied. "It's crazy."

Instead of dispersing down the block onto Broadway and Times Square, the exiting crowd had moved to the left of the theater marquee, joining the waiting mob already assembled. They blocked the sidewalk, and except for a narrow single lane of slowly moving traffic, the street as well.

I managed to station myself between two parked cars, just a few yards from the stage door. Next to me, an older man, 50 or so, smiled and said, "What did you think of the performance?"

"Fascinating," I replied. "I've never seen *Hamlet* interpreted quite that way." Richard Burton was in town, and his performance as the Danish prince was SRO. Dressed throughout the play in a black sweater and black slacks, Burton projected Hamlet as a man in complete control, forceful, undone more by circumstance than indecisiveness. He was electrifying, his voice magnificent.

As the limited New York run continued (it eventually set a record for consecutive Broadway performances of a Shakespeare play), so too did the after-show crowds multiply. Were they there to see and cheer Burton as he left the theater? Perhaps. A more probable explanation is that they wanted to catch a glimpse of his brand-new wife, Miss Elizabeth Taylor.

The scandalous goings-on of Liz 'n Dick, dating back to those weeks in Rome a couple of years earlier, had become worldwide headlines, their every move documented by fevered tabloid writers and hordes of relentless paparazzi. Their recent surprise marriage during the Toronto tryouts of Hamlet only added to the aura of glamour and notoriety that the very mention of their names evoked.

"Maybe she's not around tonight," I said after we'd waited another fifteen minutes. Taylor reportedly showed up at the theater after most, though not all, performances.

"She's inside all right," a little man in a red beret next to me said. "She got here about an hour ago."

With that, there was some movement at the stage door. Several police on foot inched closer, forming a cordon of sorts, and a burly man (bodyguard?) dressed in black opened the rear door of one of the limos next to me.

"You'll have to move back as soon as they come out," one of the cops told us. He spoke as though he'd said this before, not in an unfriendly way, but as part of his nightly routine. In fact, the hum of the big car's running motor did make me inch a bit more onto the sidewalk.

Burton appeared first. Shorter and younger-looking than I expected, he had piercing blue eyes and pockmarked skin. He smiled as the noise of the crowd grew to a roar. The din was terrific, a mix of cheering, applause, and the occasional "Richard!"

Turning, he extended his hand, and, sure enough, like a sorcerer's magical creation, *she* materialized at the open stage door. The crowd, at least those in the background, went wild. Those of us up close, on the other hand, became strangely silent.

My initial impression was that she was tiny; my second, that she was impeccably groomed; and my third, that the face I was gazing at was so beautiful I couldn't believe it belonged to a real person. Dressed in a pale pink suit and white blouse, her shiny black hair pulled back in a simple twist, Taylor was riveting, like a tinted cameo come to life. Her features were classically proportioned, her eyes a shade of violet I'd never seen before. When she turned left or right, her perfect profile was outlined against the dark blue of the uniforms of the police protecting her.

Walking slowly behind Burton towards the car, she smiled serenely, waving one half-raised arm ever so slightly. She'd once said, "I can't remember ever not being famous." The harshness of the lights of several flashbulbs only highlighted the glow of her flawless skin.

In a matter of seconds, she'd reached the car and, helped by the fellow who'd initially opened the door, she followed Burton into the back seat. Two cops on motorcycles suddenly appeared, and, like a carefully rehearsed scene from a movie, the car slowly moved away, escorted by a wailing cruiser and the two bikes.

The crowd began to thin, and I made my way to the subway—the West Side IRT local—grimy, noisy, and hot, even on this spring night. I thought about Burton's take on Hamlet as the train careened through the dark and dank turn-of-the-century tunnels, but mostly it was Taylor's ethereal beauty that rose like a pink cloud in the imaginary bubble above my head. I wondered what it would be like to have such extraordinary looks that you literally stopped traffic wherever you went.

I was in graduate school at Columbia that year, and when I got home to my apartment on West 101st Street, my roommate Charlie was still studying. I told him about my experience and a bit about the play. The next night he was in Midtown and "just happened" to stroll over to West 45th Street when the shows were letting out. When he got home later, he rushed into the apartment, and the first thing he said to me was "I saw her!" Such was the power of the impression she made.

James Agee, author of *A Death in the Family* and *Let Us Now Praise Famous Men*, and an equally distinguished film critic, wrote about the young Taylor in a review of her breakthrough movie, *National Velvet*: "She strikes me...as being rapturously beautiful."

Legendary screenwriter Joseph L. Mankiewicz, her director in *Suddenly, Last Summer* and *Cleopatra*, said, "She was the most incredible vision of loveliness I have ever seen in my life."

Mine, too.

Where I Was When
the Lights Went Out

At one time or another, we've all slogged our way through an electric power failure, but the particular outage I'm thinking about was an event of gigantic, unparalleled proportions.

I'm remembering the mother of them all, the Great Northeast Blackout of 1965. Beginning at the peak of a weekday rush hour, this monumental snafu affected millions of people from southern Canada to halfway down the Eastern Seaboard.

On Tuesday, November 9, 1965, I was having an early dinner with two friends in their ground-floor apartment on the Upper East Side of Manhattan. Our conversation had initially centered that night on a young seminarian who had set himself on fire earlier in the day at the United Nations as a protest against the government's rapidly escalating Vietnam War. He would succumb the next afternoon to his burns, his tragic demise wiped off the front page by coverage of the results of another kind of "power" failure.

Sometime before 6 pm, as our meal was cooking, the power in the apartment suddenly died. A quick look out the window confirmed that we weren't the only folks affected. Except for the headlights of cars slowly making their way down the narrow one-way street, East 87th seemed to be totally dark. An enterprising doorman in the apartment building directly opposite was already using his flashlight to hail a cab.

After several minutes of bumping into furniture and scurrying for candles, we became curious about what was happening on the avenues at each end of the block. I stepped out onto to the street and walked the short distance west to Madison. Instead of the panorama of far-off lights in the apartment towers across the expanse of Central Park, there was complete darkness.

I briefly took in the chaos of the headlights and horns of hundreds of cars crawling up the avenue from as far south as I could see and then raced back to the apartment. "The West Side is out, too!" I yelled as I stumbled through the door. "Who has a portable radio?"

My hosts found a pink plastic beach transistor, and we flipped it on. After an onslaught of static as we tried to adjust the tuner and antenna, we picked up a station from upstate Rochester operating on a local generator. Hearing shortly thereafter that the blackout extended from Toronto down into the mid-Atlantic states was sobering news, especially since its cause was apparently not yet understood. Or perhaps they weren't telling us what was really going on.

We fortified ourselves with sweaters and added an extra bottle or two of wine to our meal. The entree was an under-baked, lukewarm lasagna, a casualty of the incapacitated stove, but the salad and bread were fine. And the wine was delicious. After a few glasses, so was the lasagna.

After dinner, armed with one flashlight, the three of us trooped east over to Park Avenue. Because it's a divided, two-way street, Park presented even more of a gridlock, but, incredibly, traffic was plodding along. On our block a couple of take-charge citizens managed to get the rest of us to coordinate our erratic arm/flashlight directives as we morphed into traffic cops. My sense was that everyone, taxi drivers included, was cooperating to make the best of a fraught situation. We were soon relieved of our duties by the arrival of a police cruiser. We marched back to the apartment, rather proud of our contribution to the cause.

News reports trickled in as more radio stations activated transmitters. We eventually learned that a malfunctioning power station near Niagara Falls had blacked out an area encompassing nearly 100,000 square miles and 50 million people. Commuting New Yorkers remained stuck underground along the miles of subway and train tracks that weave in and out of the four largest boroughs. We wondered about people suspended in elevators in office skyscrapers— remember, the blackout had hit just after the end of the workday.

The hour grew late, and the novelty wore off. We'd had a few after-dinner libations, and there was no anticipated return to power anytime soon. Tomorrow, presumably, would be another workday. Around midnight, despite my friends' entreaties to sleep over, I decided to head out into the night for home.

I was living at the time on Gramercy Park, about 70 blocks and three miles to the south. By now, traffic had eased, even on Fifth Avenue, and there was a full moon shining down from an exceptionally clear sky. The temperature was in the low 40s, not that cold for November. I was 24 at the time, and I loved to trek all over Manhattan. I decided to walk.

I began by hiking jauntily down the avenue, soon passing the massive exterior of the Metropolitan Museum of Art. I marched by the darkened limestone Beaux-Arts mansion that houses the Frick Collection, another 15 blocks south.

When I reached the Plaza Hotel at 59th Street, I'd had enough of that drill. I was only halfway home, and it was now past midnight.

I managed to hail a cab already occupied by three other passengers. I recall that one rider told us she'd spent hours in a crowded elevator before being hoisted out through an emergency hatch to the floor above. This was well before cell phones became attached to our bodies, so many—perhaps most—people wouldn't have known why they were trapped wherever they happened to be when the lights went out.

We were a chatty group as we proceeded slowly down Fifth Avenue, noisily sharing our respective blackout stories. I said goodbye to my new friends and exited the cab near my apartment on the park. Circling the black wrought iron fence that encloses this small oasis of 19th-century greenery, I could see flickers of candlelight in several of the windows of the converted brownstones and mansions around Gramercy Square. Tonight, had there been gas lamps glowing instead of no lights at all, I'd have imagined myself back in the New York of Henry James.

My building was a former townhouse remodeled into two large studios per floor. I unlocked the outer door—and then, of course, found myself in total darkness. I hadn't brought along matches, but I knew the plan of the small foyer well enough to feel my way past the disabled elevator to the staircase beyond.

It's hard to explain if you haven't experienced it, sober or otherwise, but there is something unusually disorienting about trying to climb stairs in absolute darkness. I found it easier and infinitely more reassuring to get down on my hands and knees and feel the steps one by one.

When I reached the first landing, I knew I had to turn a sharp corner before I'd arrive at the steps that led to the next floor. I slowly made my way forward along the hall by feeling the wall and my neighbors' doors until the next staircase began.

Somewhere between the second floor and the next level of stairs (or two?), I lost my bearings. Had I really arrived on my level (four) or had I somehow miscalculated and made my way to the fifth floor? Or was I still on the third?

Not a big problem, one might assume. Just try your key in what you think is your door; if it's not your apartment, the key won't work. But it was a weeknight and very late. As a relatively new tenant in the building, I was reluctant to disturb my neighbors, only a couple of whom I'd even met. I convinced myself that the only way I could be certain of where to go was to retrace my steps all the way down to the entrance door and start over.

Funny? Yes, in retrospect. At the time, however, I think I experienced what must be the closest I've ever come to a panic attack. I was sweating profusely and close to tears. I seriously considered curling up on the floor in a corner and going to sleep for the remainder of the night, but I was too agitated and, besides, I really had to use the bathroom.

So back I went, this time pretty much on my hands and knees all the way. I initially tried to descend by sitting face forward and bumping down one step at a time, but that technique proved noisy and I was afraid I'd lose my balance and pitch forward. I finally had to turn and carefully inch down backwards.

I reached the ground floor and, like the intrepid mountaineer George Mallory on Mount Everest, began my upward trek once again. On this attempt, I concentrated on nothing but remembering how many times I turned on each landing and how many short hallways I navigated as I ascended to the next level.

When I finally felt the key click in my door, I stumbled in and proceeded rapidly (but carefully), arms outstretched, to the bathroom. I then got out of my sweat-soaked clothes, took a brief, cold, barely trickling shower, turned the bedroom wall switch and the radio alarm to "on," and fell asleep. Sometime toward dawn, I was awakened by the lights going on and the voice of a local DJ beginning what were to be hours of nonstop coverage of the monumental outage.

I, of course, had my own little story to tell. It got a lot of play at parties I attended in the weeks to come, complete with a dramatic re-enactment of how to crawl two different ways in total darkness, up the stairs and down. I had everyone in stitches.

One sad and chilling postscript to this tale: About a week after the blackout I found out that one of my neighbors, an older man I'd never encountered, had committed suicide sometime on November 9. He hadn't been discovered for a couple of days. I still occasionally wonder if he was already dead or still alive when I stumbled past his door that dark night.

Nickel Afternoons
on the Staten Island Ferry

It's impossible not to feel the rush of excitement as a blast from its foghorn announces the departure of the Staten Island Ferry on its short trek across New York harbor.

The startling, seemingly one-dimensional backdrop of Wall Street skyscrapers...the familiar but always stirring ride past the Statue of Liberty...the silvery cables of the majestic Verrazano-Narrows bridge spanning the entrance to the perfectly situated harbor.... All combine to evoke the dynamic presence of a city that began as a small Dutch settlement and rose to become the symbol of American opportunity, commerce, and modernity. The squawking of gulls adds a certain seafaring charm to the scene, but it's the grandeur and vitality of the metropolis that most impress.

I used to think of the Staten Island Ferry as one of my "secret places," an odd way, perhaps, to describe an everyday phenomenon shared by thousands of tourists and commuting New Yorkers. However, during my forays on the ferry, somewhere in the chaos of camera-clicking visitors, intrepid backpackers, and office workers buried in the Daily

News, I always managed to find moments of solitude and peaceful contemplation.

There has been ferry service since pre-Revolutionary War days. The city of New York took over the private Manhattan-Staten Island route in the early 1900s, gradually raising the fare to a nickel—the amount I first remember—until an increase to a dime in 1971. Now the ferry ride is free, a wondrous anomaly in a city where a studio apartment can go for $2,000-plus a month.

Sometimes I'd take out-of-town guests on the ferry, especially on Sunday excursions during summer vacation. In addition to the unsurpassed visuals in every direction, it seemed there was always a breeze blowing in 'from the Narrows and across the strait to the mouth of the Hudson River.

I didn't depend on a crowd to enjoy sailing across the harbor to Staten Island, however, so I'd occasionally ride the subway down to the Battery by myself. If the weather was nice in any of the four seasons, I liked to find a seat on the deck, sometimes a challenge between June and August but not in the cooler months. In cold weather I'd sometimes have the bench to myself. On really foggy days it was fun to guess at the location of landmarks as we chugged through the murky harbor. On those afternoons, it was easy enough to let the mind wander and imagine that we were sailing ·through uncharted waters.

Disembarking at St. George Terminal on Staten Island, I'd immediately re-board a waiting ferry for the return trip. Simply staying on was prohibited, but there was always another boat waiting to receive passengers for the half-hour voyage back. Regrettably, I never ventured on foot beyond the terminal to find out what else this least-known of the five boroughs might offer.

I did, however, have an opportunity to drive around Staten Island when I taught a few classes for a private remedial reading company I worked for during and directly after my graduate studies. These programs were conducted at two Catholic girls' schools, St. Louis Academy and the extravagantly named Our Lady Star of the Sea (a translation of a Latin name for the Virgin, Stella Maris). Both schools were situated over near the Goethals Bridge to New Jersey. This was considered the rural side of the island, big stretches of farmland belying the fact that were still in the city of New York.

This sense of remove from the metropolis seemed to pertain to the inhabitants as well, at least those I met. I remember being shocked one day to discover that several of the neatly uniformed and shy teenagers in my class had never set foot on the island of Manhattan. "Never? Ever?" I recall asking incredulously, momentarily losing my teacher cool. But I digress.

Despite the cacophony of the summer passenger scene and the constant maritime traffic in the harbor (there were always several ferries and other craft chugging in one direction or another), I found the ride to be calming in an outdoorsy, exhilarating sort of way. Aware of the surrounding activity and the constant breeze and, depending on the weather, the sun or mist on my face, I nevertheless somehow felt a bit apart and quite able to close my eyes occasionally and drift into restful reverie.

Always on the return trip, however, there was a point when I focused on the approaching tip of lower Manhattan, with those skyscrapers rising improbably, spectacularly, from—it seemed—the very edge of the shore. Invariably, there were always those few moments before we anchored when the well-worn sides of the ferry would seem to groan and then bang ominously against the aging pilings on either side of the narrow docking area.

I've not referred to the World Trade Center in lower Manhattan as part of my harbor experience, because it wasn't. The twin towers were not there when I lived in New York, then they were, and then they weren't.

After 9/11, I wondered how it seemed to commuters who traveled back and forth on the ferry in the late summer of 2001 to see the buildings standing tall one day and completely gone the next. I wonder now how it feels to gaze at the recently completed single tower rising so very high in the sky, once again dominating the lower western side of the island.

Alone in the Dark

The lights go down....the curtain parts....a flicker appears on the blank screen....and suddenly the majestic head of a lion, emitting equally regal roars, fills the emptiness around me...

I spent a good part of my life in New York transfixed and transformed by the images projected on the screens of the many movie theaters—uptown and downtown, elegant and funky, tiny and cavernous—that I frequented. I haunted these houses, usually several times a week, for many years.

I can't remember a time I didn't love the movies. Growing up in Springfield, Massachusetts, I knew every theater in town, from the eight situated in the Main Street area to a couple located within walking distance of my neighborhood. In those more innocent days, by the time I was nine or ten I was riding alone—my preference—on the downtown bus to catch the latest Betty Grable musical or Roy Rogers western.

In college, a decade later, I discovered foreign films at the venerable Avon Theater—still going strong—on Thayer Street in Providence, Rhode Island, and I engaged in heady debates late into the night about symbolism and such in Bergman and Fellini, Kurosawa and Truffaut. I did manage, however, to walk down the hill, often, to the opulent Loew's State or RKO Albee for lighter fare starring the likes of Doris Day and William Holden.

Landing in New York in 1963, however, I found true Nirvana, a cinema Shangri-La of first-run features, revivals, foreign films, and even theaters specializing in genres such as the musical and the avant-garde. It was movie heaven for someone who, as a kid, had devoured the pages of monthlies such as *Modern Screen*, *Movie Mirror*, and the ultimate in fan mags, the glossy *Photoplay*.

I caught current first-run and so-called "art" films (a fancy name for the more seriously reviewed movies) at the classy Rugoff chain (Cinemas I and II, the Beekman, Plaza, Gramercy, and several other small venues). Although primarily situated on the affluent East Side, these theaters all offered special student discounts of 50 percent via ID cards and strips of perforated coupons, both of which I carried in my wallet in case the urge to see a flick unexpectedly overcame me. That discount meant I could see a first-run film for $2, tops. Prices were even cheaper at the repertory houses.

My most memorable film-going experiences did in fact occur at the various rep theaters located all over the city, especially on the Upper West Side and in the Village. These houses usually featured films from the past, many of which only the most devoted aficionado would even know, much less see and appreciate.

Those are the theaters I imagined the great film critic Pauline Kael was really talking about when she said in *For Keeps: 30 Years at the Movies*: "Sitting there alone... you know there must be others perhaps in this very theater or in this city, surely in other theaters in other cities, now, in the past or future, who react as you do." I understood exactly what Kael was saying; I knew I was one of those "others." Kael's followers, by the way, became known as "Paulettes," though I don't recall any of my film friends actually addressing me that way. Other names, perhaps, but not "Paulette."

It didn't take me long after my arrival at Columbia in the fall of '63 to discover the Thalia, a small, somewhat dingy repertory theater at Broadway and 95th Street. A few blocks south of my first Manhattan apartment, the Thalia became my go-to mini-movie palace, the place where I saw, literally, hundreds of films ranging from Charlie Chaplin double features to classics of film noir to foreign gems of the post-war years to early, non-mainstream American efforts by up-and-coming directors like Martin Scorsese.

Part of the appeal of the Thalia was that they generally changed the double bill every day. In hindsight, given the rental costs, scheduling, and the possible complications from undelivered or otherwise unavailable prints, this policy seems grandly ambitious. To me it meant having weekly access to a trove of cinema treasures. If I didn't like today's bill of fare, tomorrow's would probably be enticing, and the next day's, a must-see.

Accommodating only a few hundred patrons, the Thalia was squeezed into the lower level of a big theater, the Symphony, that faced Broadway. You entered the Thalia under a small, curved marquee around the corner on 95th. If you ever happen to catch a showing of Woody Allen's *Annie Hall*, there is an exterior shot of that little marquee advertising Marcel Ophuls' four-hour *The Sorrow and the Pity*. Designed in a vaguely Art Deco motif that had seen better days, the interior had an odd layout—very narrow, with a slight upwards slope *toward* the screen, disconcerting if those in the front rows were tall or moved around a lot. Smoking in those days was permitted in the back rows.

Often a line would form outside the theater between the continuous showings, and I recall having lively conversations with like-minded strangers as we discussed the merits of the films we were about to see or those from a few days earlier. Sometimes we'd sit together, and, occasionally, a friendship of one kind or another might develop from these encounters. Meeting and conversing with a like-minded movie devotee did create, after all, an instant and not inconsiderable bond.

And the Thalia did abound in true film fanatics. If anything went slightly askew in the projection room, it wasn't long before shouts of "Turn up the sound!" or "Focus, goddammit!" served to fix the problem before more than a few precious frames unreeled. This was a different kind of audience participation from what I remember as a kid attending kiddie matinees back in Springfield, but no less vociferous.

It wasn't long before I discovered other theaters around town that catered to the serious filmgoer. Part of me did miss my childhood experience of seeing, in one sitting, a second-run "B" film, followed by a newsreel, cartoon, the always welcome previews of coming attractions and, finally, the first-run feature. But that was then, and now I was becoming a seasoned student of the cinema, able on any night to watch an uncut classic for the first time.

I'd seen a few of these golden oldies, unmercifully chopped and truncated, on late-late TV shows, interrupted every few minutes by high-volume commercials, and I occasionally watched the New York-based Million Dollar Movie, with its introductory "Tara's Theme" from *Gone with the Wind*. But now I was enjoying these classics as the director had really envisioned.

Theatre 80 St. Mark's, down in the East Village, was a subway ride followed by a longish walk, but its programming was worth the schlep. The St. Mark's showed mostly vintage musicals in its tiny space, originally a speakeasy and later a jazz club. Posters of movie musicals and autographed photos of the likes of Katharine Hepburn, Gloria Swanson, Bette Davis, and Henry Fonda adorned the lobby walls. None of them was particularly noted for singing and dancing skills, but hey, they were big movie stars.

At the St. Mark's, I had the chance to view seldom seen films from the old Hollywood dream factory, song-filled classics like Ernst Lubitsch's *The Merry Widow* and Vincente Minnelli's *Cabin in the Sky*, with Ethel Waters and Lena Horne, one of the few big studio films of its time with an all African-American cast. That film also featured Butterfly McQueen, for once not playing the stereotypical ninny we best remember from *Gone with the Wind*.

Other movie houses I frequented were the Bleecker Street in the Village and the Carnegie Hall Cinema, situated underneath the legendary hall itself. Occasionally, I went to the latter with a friend whose house manager mother got us in for free. The Regency on upper Broadway I remember for the restored black-and-white film prints that were wonderfully sharp and clear. A few blocks north, the New Yorker had exceptional pairings of foreign films. Like the Thalia, their schedule was chock full of ever-changing double bills. The New Yorker looms large in my memory because I always checked to see what was on as I rode past its large marquee on the 104 Broadway bus that ran from 42nd Street all the way up to West Harlem.

Down in the Chelsea area at the old Elgin (later a porno site and now the Joyce, a leading dance venue), I remember being totally mesmerized by F. W. Murnau's silent film *Sunrise*, often included on lists of all-time greatest films. As the last shot dissolved from the reunited lovers to a blazing sun, the audience erupted in wild applause. I had not experienced that before in a movie theater, but I did again, several times, in succeeding years. That spontaneous applause for an exceptional film was always a thrilling moment, but never more so than that first-time experience with *Sunrise*.

Such was my passion for the movies that I seriously considered getting a second master's degree, this in film studies. I took classes at Columbia, where Andrew Sarris, estimable film critic at the *Village Voice*, taught. I faithfully read Pauline Kael's column in *The New Yorker*, and, before her, Judith Crist in the *Herald Trib*une and *New York Magazine*. I discovered the collected movie reviews of James Agee, the best film critic of them all.

I even had several conversations with Dwight Macdonald, who wrote a review column for *Esquire* and lived upstairs from a friend on East 87th Street. In the end I opted for, I suppose, the job security of a library science degree. The more adventurous path of a film critic remains one of my roads not taken.

Nowadays, with the advent of TV channels like American Movie Classics and Turner Classic Movies, not to mention the easy access to restored films on DVD, the repertory theater has seen its day, certainly in smaller cities. There are new art movie houses in Manhattan, however, and programs within museums and on college campuses that continue the tradition, albeit on a smaller and less commercial scale.

Martin Scorsese once said in an interview, "The Thalia was better than film school. It's where I learned about film." For me, the Thalia and those other houses were a major part of my own non-academic education as a young man living in New York. Seeing all those films with other eager and engaged enthusiasts was an experience like no other. We were alone, yet together, in the dark.

Up against the Wall! Part I: Columbia 1968

W hen I arrived in New York in August 1963 to attend graduate school at Columbia, I never thought I'd stay for 18 years. However, once I'd tasted life in Gotham, the Big Apple, the city that never sleeps, I was hooked. Had I not had good reasons to return to New England in 1981, I'm not sure I'd have ever left. But that's another story.

In 1968 I was living in a brownstone on West 103rd Street, near the Hudson and a short walk to the Columbia campus. No longer a student there since finishing my master's degree in American Literature in 1964, I'd been teaching English at a variety of private high schools.

I first became aware of some sort of disturbance on campus one balmy night in late April. Rachel, a friend who was still in grad school, called and told me she'd heard through the grapevine that what had begun as a small demonstration earlier that day was gathering steam. "They're going for an all-out takeover," she told me. "How am I going to get into the library?" I agreed to meet her in an hour at the main entrance to the campus.

It was hard to tell if anything unusual was going on as I walked up Broadway from my apartment. Traffic—passenger cars, speeding taxis, delivery trucks, and wheezing city transit buses—was chaotic, but that was normal. Drivers and pedestrians vied to beat the lights at every block, cabbies yelled, buses honked at double-parked cars.

As I reached the environs of the campus, however, I heard loudspeakers. Soon I could see police cars, their emergency lights flashing in the twilight, lined up along Broadway at the main gates, just opposite the 116th Street subway entrance. Traffic was nearly at a halt, and some cars were being diverted down side streets. I noticed a few big vans from local TV stations parked near the gates.

I spotted Rachel, dwarfed by a big brown police horse, its rider's demeanor impassive and his eyes hidden by sunglasses. Rachel, wearing what I called her Left Bank beret, was loaded down with books. She had a worried look on her face.

"Now they're taking over some of the buildings," she told me. "I won't be able to get to my class at Hamilton, and they've even gotten into Low." Low Library, the massive, domed McKim, Mead, and White edifice rising above broad steps on the main quad, was the central administrative building. Here were located the offices of the president and others high up in the Columbia hierarchy.

"Do you still carry your ID?" Rachel asked. I did, in fact, have my old student card in my wallet. I still used it fairly often to get reduced admission to museums and such.

I nodded. "Can you walk with me to Butler?" she asked. "I need to return these books and get some reserve stuff, and they're not letting anyone into the campus without a Columbia ID."

That kind of security had not happened in my memory, but, sure enough, we had to flash our cards at a harried campus officer guarding the massive black iron gates, now nearly closed. We made our way into the quad, mobbed with students and probably others who'd gotten in before they started checking identities. On our left, the steps of Low were full, some students holding banners that said "STRIKE!," a few waving red flags. Demonstrators crowded around the imposing bronze statue of Alma Mater, seated, her arms outstretched in benevolent, gracious welcome.

Other students crowded around the sundial on College Walk, which bisects the huge quad. On the opposite side, the wide walkways leading to Butler Library were equally crowded (Butler was the actual main library, where I was to work for a decade a few years later). Hundreds of red tulips recently planted in the center strip seemed to be holding up, though I wondered how long that would last. We made our way to the library entrance, beneath the massive inscriptions of the names of Homer, Plato, Dante, Shakespeare, and other dead white male literary luminaries.

"I'm going in," Rachel said. "Seth's coming over later." Seth was Rachel's boyfriend, also a grad student.

"Call me with the latest," I said, "maybe we can have dinner at Tom's." Tom's was a cheap but good corner restaurant/deli a couple of blocks down on Broadway where

I'd had hundreds of meals during my years as a student and neighborhood resident.

"OK, but everything seems to be under control," Rachel answered as she disappeared into the library. By the next time we talked, all that would have changed.

Dusk had come, and the lights in the high Doric-columned windows of Butler were now ablaze in their usual yellow-greenish glow. I turned and walked back over toward Low, where someone with a megaphone was speaking. I couldn't make out the words. Lights from TV crews scattered here and there were blinding in their intensity, and radios blared from the upper windows of the dorms bordering Broadway and Amsterdam Avenue.

To me, an observer, the scene was disorienting. This was not the Columbia I knew, and I felt uneasiness at what was clearly the seriousness of the demonstrators. On the surface, it was an event, a happening, but there was a palpable undercurrent of urgency and determination.

So, what was the commotion all about? The immediate impetus for the uprising involved the construction of a gymnasium on the slope of Morningside Park, which forms the border between Columbia and Harlem. The University had a long history of problems with its neighbors on the Upper West Side of Manhattan, but nowhere was the split between the ivory tower and the locals more pronounced than here. A steep incline in the terrain of the park actually separates the heights from the avenues and numbered streets of Harlem down below.

Although Columbia had decided to build two gyms, one on the top for the academic population, another at the base for the neighborhood, this plan was seen as demeaning and condescending to the mostly Black residents of Harlem. For weeks, increasingly passionate speeches and gatherings had taken place on campus, and the first real action of the uprising was the tearing down by students of the construction fence at the base of the park.

Though I hadn't particularly kept up with happenings on the Columbia campus since my recent student days, I and everyone else that spring were more than aware that we were living in tumultuous and dangerous times. Martin Luther King had been assassinated a few weeks earlier, with Robert Kennedy's murder to follow in June. The Vietnam War dragged on, increasingly unpopular and morally questionable (the My Lai massacre had just occurred in March). I suspect the gymnasium controversy was the push that tipped the already rocky foundation on which authority—political, academic, and social—was tottering.

I'd been treated well by Columbia a few years earlier, when they registered me for an extra year of thesis work, thereby qualifying me for yet another Selective Service student deferment from the draft pool. Rumor had it, however, that the university was now reporting undergraduate class standings to local draft boards, which were eager to increase the volume of eligible draftees for deployment to Southeast Asia. Columbia also apparently had a close, somewhat murky relationship with the Institute for Defense Analysis at the Pentagon.

I hung around for a while that night, listening to various student speakers, among them Mark Rudd, who had already gained some notoriety from previous demonstrations by the

SDS (Students for a Democratic Society). Someone shouted into a loudspeaker that Low Library was now "officially" occupied, including the office of the president, Grayson Kirk.

Scattered groups of students chanted "Kirk must go!" and "Kirk is a jerk!" Their affect was that anomalous blend of gravity and exhilaration that seemed to characterize, at least so far, the entire demonstration. However, over at nearby Hamilton Hall, the undergraduate building, the dean had actually been taken hostage, and students, mostly Black members of the Afro-American Society, leaned out the windows, some of them raising their hands in victory signs.

Over the next several days, I visited the campus in the late afternoon on the way home from my teaching job near Lincoln Center, or later on in the evening. By now the media coverage was intense, and the organizational efforts of the students much more evident. Identical red flags flew from the five buildings now taken over and occupied. Many demonstrators wore armbands: red for the strikers, green for those advocating amnesty for the students, blue indicating a nonviolent approach, and white for faculty supporters.

One night about two or three days into the riot, a young female student, probably a Barnard undergrad, handed me a black, red, and white "STRIKE!" button as I arrived on campus. Others, blue and white (the Columbia colors), read, "Strike If We Must." I took the button but was nervous about wearing it without an identifying armband, since several outsiders had been arrested for trespassing. I stuffed it into my pocket.

Electricity and water had been turned off in the occupied buildings, though I believe drinking water was periodically brought in. Food supplies were provided to some extent, but by the fourth day or so, supporters were tossing bags into the open windows or to students perched on second-floor overhangs. I saw a big guy expertly throwing packages of fried chicken through the large windows of Low Library. Nearly every one of those chickens reached their destination, amid the cheers of both occupying students inside and onlookers milling in the plaza.

On what turned out to be the last night of the insurrection, I sensed a different mood on campus. There were just as many demonstrators and onlookers, both on the streets and inside the gates. The music was as pervasive, the loudspeakers as active. But litter was now everywhere, and it was difficult to avoid stepping in the droppings deposited by the huge horses of New York's Finest. The number of police seemed to have escalated, and I noted that many of them were wearing motorcycle-type helmets with visors. So-called "talks" between the strikers and the administration had been going on for days, but the word was that not much had been accomplished. President Kirk was maintaining a stance of distance and rigidity.

For me there was a sense that night that something had to give, that something had to happen. There had been rumors that the city police, already present in considerable numbers, would soon be removing, by force if necessary, the students in the occupied buildings. Such action, however, was seen as a drastic, last-ditch maneuver, contrary in spirit and tradition to what the private campus stood for and what the university represented.

I walked home with strangely mixed feelings. On the one hand, I was young enough and close enough to my own grad student days to feel the excitement of participation, of taking control, of doing something to express anger and outrage at what was happening in the world. And yet my earlier days as an undergraduate had involved no student demonstrations or overt protests of any kind. As a World War II baby, I straddled the last of the Fifties generation in postwar America, for whom peace, prosperity and maintaining the status quo were de rigueur. I guess I didn't quite know where I fit in, and that realization was disquieting and even depressing to me.

Early the next morning, I was awakened by a phone call from Rachel. We'd talked during the week, but today she sounded shaken. "They stormed us last night, hundreds of cops. Seth's here in the hospital. I'm calling from a pay phone in the lobby."

Rachel went on to explain what had happened. "I told you that Seth had gotten 'way involved. I was afraid he'd do something crazy so I've been going with him to the campus. Late last night, in they stormed. Hundreds of cops." Later it was estimated that 1,000 specially trained police were dispatched around 2 am to remove the students from the occupied buildings.

"Police vans were lined up all along Broadway," Rachel continued. "The cops started moving onto College Walk. They gave another warning, and then when no one came out, they charged the buildings. They all had helmets and flashlights and clubs. It was horrible." Police had also entered some of the buildings through the maze of tunnels that crisscrosses the campus, with maps presumably supplied by the administration.

Rachel told me that when they saw people being dragged out of the buildings, those in the plaza panicked. "Seth grabbed me and we started to run down the steps to College Walk. We could hear people screaming. I turned around and saw cops dragging people all the way down by their feet. Their heads were banging on the steps. Others they just grabbed and started clubbing."

"Wait, wait, are you OK?" I yelled into the phone.

"Yes, I'm all right." She laughed, a bit hysterically. "We all ran out the gates and across Broadway down 116th Street toward Riverside. There were lots of cops behind us. You could hear the clomping of the horses on the pavement. That was really scary. I got separated from Seth and crouched in a doorway, and they galloped past me. Seth fell under a streetlight, and a cop ran up to him and started hitting him on the back and head with his club."

Rachel paused and then, her voice rising, continued on. "I couldn't help it, I ran up to them screaming. By then I think Seth was unconscious, and the cop yelled for someone to get an ambulance. When it came, I ran behind it over to St. Luke's and found him in the emergency room. He came to, but he's in surgery or having stitches or something. They said he'd be OK."

"What about you?" I asked again. "Did anyone hit you?" By now I was fully awake, but I still couldn't comprehend what had happened.

"I have a bruise on my face, but I think I fell. I lost my sweater and my beret you always joke about. And my clothes are all bloody from Seth's head. Listen, I've got to get back to the waiting room." She hung up.

I couldn't go back to sleep after Rachel's call, so I got dressed for work and walked up Broadway. It was a cool and misty morning, and the campus was eerily quiet and nearly deserted. There were a couple of cops standing guard, so I flashed my ID and they let me through, maybe because I was wearing a jacket and tie.

The grounds were still a mess—paper all over the place, bottles on the grass and in the bushes, trash baskets askew. Out on Broadway a heavy wood and metal bench on the median strip had somehow been uprooted from the cement.

Over at the mathematics building, a big black and white "Liberated Zone" sign still hung from the upper floor. Nearly all the tulips on the long path to Butler Library had been trampled, their red petals nearly buried in the brown soil. There was no music playing. I walked out to the entrance to the subway stop, fished a token out of my pocket, and grabbed a downtown local to the school at Lincoln Center where I taught.

A few days later, on the weekend, I returned to the campus, stopping at the Chock Full o'Nuts restaurant across from the main gates for a cup of coffee to go. The television and newspaper coverage of the uprising had been extensive, and we'd read a lot of statistics: Besides the 1,000 tactical force police who stormed the buildings, 700 civilians— some students, others not—had been arrested, and more than

54

200 actually taken to hospitals around the city for injuries. Hundreds of others had been hurt but did not seek treatment.

Coffee in hand, I walked over to the statue of Alma Mater to examine a sign propped in her lap. It read, "Raped by the Police." All the litter was gone by now, and there was more of a sense of normalcy. Had this been any other Saturday in early May, I'm not sure I'd have noticed much, except for the sign, that was different. Buildings and Grounds workers were already completing the replanting of hundreds of red tulips, just in time for the upcoming graduation.

Many classes had been canceled for the rest of the semester, however, and no final exams were being held. The following week another strike occurred, but this was of short duration. Construction of the Morningside Heights gymnasium was completely halted and plans eventually shelved.

Commencement was held that year in the massive Cathedral of St. John the Divine, a few blocks away. Several hundred students stood up in protest and filed out of the cathedral at a predetermined time. They walked back to the campus and had their own graduation seated on the steps of Low Library, cheered on by over a thousand spectators on College Walk.

During the summer, Grayson Kirk, who had succeeded General Dwight Eisenhower as President of Columbia, resigned, his tenure of 15 years irrevocably damaged by his behavior—reactive and uncompromising—during the strike. When Kirk's name is mentioned now, it's always in connection with the events of the spring of 1968.

The fabric of a great university—my university—had been tarnished as well. Inaction, lack of empathy, and, in the end, an inappropriate show of brute force had shaken to its very foundation the ivory tower on Morningside Heights.

A Pigeon Cooed in Gramercy Park

The closest I came to living in a New York neighborhood that reminds me of my favorite city, London, was when I rented an apartment down on Gramercy Park. OK, it was a small studio that faced the back alley of another building, but when I stepped out the front door onto Gramercy Park South, I was occasionally tempted to warble a chorus of that old World War II standard, "A Nightingale Sang in Berkeley Square."

Gramercy Park, two blissful acres of cultivated greenery in the heart of Manhattan, is located above the East Village between 20th and 21st Streets, bisecting Lexington Avenue to the north and Irving Place to the south. Despite a few inroads of condos and renovated brownstones over the years, the park and its environs retain a powerful feel of the 19th century. On a foggy night, with the period street lamps emitting a soft glow and the square bereft of passersby and traffic, it's not difficult to conjure up the inviting clip-clop of horses' hooves or, depending on your mood, a midnight scene out of *Dr. Jekyll and Mr. Hyde*.

I lived on the park shortly after the area was formally declared a historic district in 1966, though over the years the owners of most of the buildings had striven, on their own and successfully, to maintain the square's original opulence and historical essence. Two notable examples are the mansions housing the National Arts Club and the Players Club (founded by the Shakespearean actor Edwin Booth). Both still stand in genteel splendor on the south side of the park.

Edwin Booth entertained visitors in his private apartment atop the Players Club. I liked to think John Wilkes Booth, his younger brother, had sometimes visited (the building sits nearly next door to where I lived) until I discovered that Edwin had bought the building in 1888, decades after John had his bloody encounter with Abraham Lincoln at Ford's Theater.

Very few spots on the island of Manhattan are so evocative of an earlier age as Gramercy Park and its surrounding structures. Henry James, a onetime resident, described the ambiance as having "the incomparable tone of time." Brass lanterns, fences with fancy grill work, gargoyles embedded in concrete facades, and massive door knockers attached to formidable front doors are fixtures of many of the houses that face the park. It's this combination of stately structures and the oasis of trees, shrubs, and carefully maintained flower beds that so strongly evokes the countless squares that characterize the landscape of London.

The park was created as a private enclave and, as such, was kept locked nearly from its beginnings in the mid-1800s. As a resident of a building bordering the square, I had a key, sort of. My landlady owner, who maintained a pied-à-terre in one of the apartments and for whom the word "eccentric" only begins to describe her mercurial behavior, would occasionally allow the tenants access to the park via the building key. I believe each owner paid a steep fee for this key, including a substantial replacement cost, a fact of which we renters were frequently reminded.

I rarely had occasion in those busy days to relax on one of the benches scattered throughout the park, so obtaining the elusive key was not a big deal for me. Though I did manage to get in during the times the owner and I were on good speaking terms, mostly I enjoyed the views from the outside.

It was pleasant to meander around the periphery and take in whatever activity was occurring behind the black wrought iron fence. I don't recall strict rules other than that involving the key, but in more recent years a park association has imposed more than a few: There is no ball-playing permitted and no feeding of the birds and squirrels. Dogs, leashed or not, are forbidden from entering the park.

I do remember that residents would gather and chat and read in the sun or shade on the benches along the flower-bordered gravel paths. In the center, a raised, larger-than-life statue of Edwin Booth, deep in contemplation as Hamlet, was a reminder of the rich heritage surrounding us. I recall the occasional small groups of supervised children. There was one nanny, in particular, whom I used to see wheeling her charge in one of those shiny midnight blue perambulators with big wheels. Very British.

It was the simple fact of just living on the park that appealed. I have to admit it was fun for me, just out of grad school, to instruct a cab driver late at night, "Gramercy

Park South!" or to watch the subtle reaction when I gave my address to a store clerk or some other New Yorker for whom the locale was synonymous with big bucks and a certain social exclusivity. Little did they know that I was inhabiting a space not much larger than the single dorm room I'd occupied a few years earlier, back in my senior year in college.

"Stretch it" was the operative phrase for my style of living back in the late 60s, and it was fortunate that there were a lot of cheap restaurants over on nearby Third Avenue or further south, toward the Village. My favorite haunt was literally just around the corner, a neighborhood bar and restaurant on Irving Place (named for Washington Irving, a supposed early street resident). The place was called Pete's Tavern. Pete's had been around forever, and its big claim to fame was as the hangout of short story writer O. Henry. Pete's, at least back when I knew it (it's a big more upscale these days), served cheap spaghetti dinners in booths with red-and-white checkered tablecloths. The big, antique bar took up virtually the entire left side of the interior.

If I had out-of-town guests and wanted to splurge, we'd head further down Irving Place to where it ended a few blocks south. There we'd dine at Luchow's, smack across the street on the south side of 14th.

Luchow's was a true Old New York institution, a sprawling restaurant with a series of ornately decorated rooms: brass chandeliers holding enormous bulbs, oak panels with carved images, big oil paintings by European masters, scores of beer steins, and a huge bar with arched stained glass windows against the wall. There were several very good, less expensive German restaurants up on East 86th Street in Yorkville, one of my future neighborhoods, but none had the opulence or panache of Luchow's.

The restaurant was at its best at Christmas, with an enormous lighted tree that rose skywards into an extended part of the ceiling of the main room. Pine wreaths and branches were tucked into nooks and crannies everywhere. In addition to feeling a sense of nostalgia for what was and is no more (the restaurant closed for good in 1983, the building demolished), I also recall the delicious wiener schnitzel, purple cabbage, and roast potatoes. This was a few years before a close friend convinced me that it was immoral to eat the carcass of a baby cow. Times and habits change.

In its early years, Luchow's was a gathering place for illustrious diners such as Diamond Jim Brady, Lillian Russell, Victor Herbert, Andrew Carnegie, and J. P. Morgan, all of whom flocked to 14th Street. In their day, 14th Street was the "Times Square" of New York—the center of the city's theatrical and musical nightlife. It's "back to 14th Street" where Dolly Levi heads at the conclusion of the blockbuster musical *Hello, Dolly*, which was still in its initial Broadway run at the time I lived on Gramercy Park South.

Another landmark on 14th Street was the Academy of Music, literally next door to Luchow's. Not to be confused with the original Academy across the street (the premier opera house in town, before the Metropolitan), this Academy of Music began as a lavish movie palace in the 1920s and later morphed into a concert hall.

Lest the reader think that my attraction to the Gramercy Park area was all about its illustrious past, I should mention that I saw The Band, the great roots rock group, play at the Academy of Music in the 60s, as well as other big names from that golden age of pop music. It was one of the premier stops on every rock icon's itinerary.

One particularly memorable visit to the Academy occurred in 1965 when I treated my then-teenage brother, Greg, to a concert by the young Rolling Stones on their very first American tour. The upper level tickets were five dollars each. Now, THAT seems like a very long time ago.

My Days and Nights at the Plaza

The elevator operator and I waited for Clint Eastwood to oblige a young autograph seeker in the lobby of the Plaza Hotel. He signed her book, said a few words, and stepped inside. The doors closed and up the three of us went.

Clint, exceedingly lanky and amiable, apologized for the delay and smiled. I smiled back. He got off and I continued on to my office. I worked at the hotel and was used to such celebrity encounters, but it was always a treat when they occurred, usually spontaneously and without fanfare.

You might wonder how I, a teacher and librarian, found myself gainfully employed by this legendary landmark, a place frequented by the rich and famous, filmed in a dozen movies, its very name synonymous with the glamour of 20th-century Manhattan. I took the job on a whim, and though my time at the Plaza spanned only a year, I made the most of it.

I was teaching English at the Professional Children's School at Lincoln Center in the late 1960s. Young and energetic and always looking for new adventures, I soon realized that, even with homework papers and class preparation, I had free time in the late afternoon and early evening.

I was also finding that if I were to keep up my theater-going activities at the rate to which I was becoming accustomed, I'd be needing some extra change. And, of course, the Plaza evoked a kind of New York that I'd only begun to know, let alone experience. One walk through the grand lobbies— lushly carpeted and festooned with gold filigree, expensive furnishings, and lavish floral arrangements—and I was hooked.

It turned out that the ad I answered was for a part-time position in the collection department, a small unit devoted to the tracking down of clients who had received services, but for a variety of reasons—some legitimate, others bogus, more than a few bizarre—had not paid their bill.

I ended up doing a bit of everything: filing, correspondence, answering the phone. The work itself was routine, but I liked my colleagues, the perks were substantial, the venue beguiling. And some of the tales I heard would have made prime fodder for the likes of Suzy Knickerbocker, Earl Wilson, and other New York gossip and society columnists of the day.

After finishing my teaching in the mid-afternoon, I'd head crosstown from Lincoln Center to the juncture of Central Park South and Fifth Avenue, where The Plaza, built in the style of a French Renaissance château, sits in regal splendor. It was a good walking distance, well over a mile, and I never tired of it.

I'd head south on Broadway, crossing busy Columbus Circle, with its namesake perched on an impressive 70-foot column, beholding a brave new world he never could have imagined. Off to the side, startling in its pristine, white marble facade, rose Huntington Hartford's Gallery of Modern Art. Designed by renowned architect Edward Durell Stone, this 12-story Venetian palazzo had been commissioned by the A&P heir to display his private art collection.

Dodging traffic, I'd continue my stroll along the northern side of Central Park South, leafy and cool in the summer, frigid and blustery in January, with winds sweeping up the canyons of the intersecting avenues from the lower reaches of the island. I liked the park side of the street because I'd be able to pass the horses waiting to take tourists on a pricey carriage ride through Central Park.

Though I never spoke to the drivers—or their horses—there were a few I came to recognize because of their distinctive headgear—feathers atop a horse's head, for example, and a top hat à la Fred Astaire for his keeper. Back then, I viewed this colorful fixture of the Midtown landscape as a picturesque part of the New York scene. Today, I tend to agree with current Mayor de Blasio's comment regarding his efforts to end the carriage rides: "The biggest and densest urban area in North America is not a place for horses."

I usually entered the hotel through the main lobby around the corner on Fifth Avenue. I liked the bustle and the noise: doormen waving and blowing whistles, yellow cabs arriving and departing, the constant movement of the revolving door. It was a quintessential New York scene, and, in fact, the inevitable opening shot for any movie featuring the hotel.

Just inside the entrance, on the left, was the Persian Room, a small nightclub where a large placard advertised the current singer in residence—perhaps Peggy Lee, Jack Jones, or Diahann Carroll. Straight ahead was the sumptuous, high-ceiling space with oversize potted plants and polished marble columns known as the Palm Court. As I approached, I'd hear the soothing strains of a violin or piano and the muffled conversation of patrons—the majority women—enjoying late afternoon high tea. This repast was aptly named, both for the lavishness of the pastries and the steep tab.

Although most of the hotel's clerical offices were in an uncomfortably cramped section of the basement, I worked with my collection department colleagues in an improvised space on the top floor of the hotel. I'd step into one of the vacant elevators and, if we were waiting for other passengers to enter, chat with the operator. I'm sure the elevator men were hired, in part, for their good looks and how well they wore their snappy uniform: emerald green jacket with gold buttons, dark slacks, and white gloves.

Riding to the top, I'd exit the elevator directly into the spacious waiting room of an advertising agency that occupied the 18th floor, then walk up a narrow flight of stairs to, essentially, the garret of the hotel. We conducted our business in a modestly renovated space adjoining many other rooms filled with old furniture, bric-à-brac, abandoned file cabinets, and cluttered service trays. I'd work with the staff for a few hours, take a break for dinner, work alone some more, and then, mid-evening, ride the subway back to my apartment on the Upper West Side.

Dinner was not a sandwich brought from home or an apple left over from my lunch at school. I got to eat, at no charge, in a basement staff cafeteria reached after a maze-like walk around and through the huge kitchens. The surroundings were not elegant, but the food most definitely was.

There were always several basic cafeteria-type dishes available, as well as simple salads and desserts. But usually— and here's what I focused on—there was a generous and varied choice of whatever was left over from the entrées offered mid-day in the upstairs restaurants, as well as fancier appetizers and desserts: English sole from the Edwardian Room; crab Rangoon, courtesy of Trader Vic's; a lamb chop from the Oak Room's hearty menu; chocolate cake that had been artfully arranged a few hours earlier on the dessert cart in the Palm Court. I ate well.

Other perks included a 50 percent reduction of the check at whatever public room I frequented. I didn't take advantage of this discount often, but I remember seeing Lainie Kazan (who had replaced Barbra Streisand in *Funny Girl* on Broadway a couple years earlier) at the Persian Room. When my mother came to the big city to visit, we occasionally sampled that fancy tea in the Palm Court.

On special occasions, I sometimes dined with friends at Trader Vic's. This restaurant, located below street level, was a recent, somewhat incongruous addition to the venerable hotel, what with its "tiki" atmosphere and ersatz Polynesian menu. The elaborate decor was pretty in a Technicolor "B" movie sort of way, with burnished lighting, a thatched roof, native carvings, and a huge outrigger canoe (salvaged from the then-recent Marlon Brando remake of *Mutiny on the Bounty*) in the lobby. The enormous drinks, several served with floating flowers, were tropical killers.

Most of my Plaza encounters with celebrities occurred in the main lobby of the hotel or, like my brief conversation with Clint Eastwood, in the elevators. Charlotte Rampling, in town, I believe, to promote the Visconti film, *The Damned*, affected a stony stare at the floor indicator during our entire ride. Tom Jones, wildly popular at the time, was friendly, as were singers Frankie Laine and, especially, Dusty Springfield, whom I spoke to briefly as she was signing autographs one day in the lobby during her engagement at the Persian Room.

One afternoon I was approaching the elevators and noticed a tiny, well-groomed woman wearing a little black veiled hat making her way to where one of the operators was waiting for a neighboring car to fill. He politely asked her to take that elevator because it was nearly ready to depart. She waved him off, entered his empty car, and turned. I immediately recognized Gloria Swanson, still looking the way she had in her big comeback picture, *Sunset Boulevard*, several years earlier. As the disconcerted fellow hesitated, she turned and commanded in her most imperious, clipped Norma Desmond voice, "Nonsense! Take me up. Now!" The door closed, and up, indeed, they went.

Royalty often stayed at the Plaza, but, though we were all well aware of the extra security, I never saw a tiara or any procession marching through the lobby. Nor did I get a glimpse during their visit of show-biz royalty Liz Taylor and

Richard Burton and their multiple trolleys of luggage and considerable entourage. The Taylor-Burton retinue occupied the better part of an entire floor. The ruckus caused by the Beatles during their several days' stay in 1964 was before my time.

The delinquent accounts handled by the collection department actually proved to be the most interesting aspect of my Plaza experience. Some were successfully resolved, others were "written off," and lots were still in limbo when I left. Many involved well-known public figures, others not so famous, but all worthy of a segment on "Lifestyles of the Rich and Famous."

I sometimes wonder what happened to the case of a titled European who refused to pay her bill, claiming her very expensive fur coat had been stolen, though there was reason, involving her equally missing gentleman companion, to believe otherwise. A ubiquitous Eastern guru who had a celebrity following (including several rock bands) ran up a large bill during the New York leg of a world tour. His people claimed it was to be paid by his "sponsors," all of whom denied responsibility.

A celebrated singer/actress, known for owing creditors all over town—including other hotels who were holding her luggage—had one of the larger files in the department. A famous World War II hero, much decorated, was in serious arrears (I believe his bill was forgiven). And one boozy night a prominent businessman toppled a large Chinese vase in one of the lobbies. He denied ever coming into physical contact with it, though witnesses remembered the collision. It was fascinating to observe how a luxury hotel has to balance a tradition of propriety, tact, deference, and goodwill regarding its illustrious clients against the acumen necessary to run a successful business.

One marketing phenomenon I never quite "got" was the promotion of Eloise, a fictional and somewhat bratty kid depicted in a series of successful books by the entertainer Kay Thompson and illustrator Hillary Knight. There were Eloise products galore available in the gift store, and a guest room was transformed into a Pepto-Bismol pink depiction of Eloise's bedroom. For a brief period, there was an Eloise ice cream bar, but that was short-lived. (I've heard, however, that in recent years Eloise has been resurrected by way of a new Eloise suite and an Eloise shop.)

Another change I witnessed was the unexpected closing of the Edwardian Room, called the Men's Café in the days of Alfred G. Vanderbilt, the very first guest to sign the hotel register on October 1, 1907. Overnight, it seemed, this elegant, wood-paneled restaurant morphed into the Green Tulip, a gaudy venue decorated in Sixties psychedelic colors, offering disco dancing and occasional folk singers. There were a lot of complaints, and soon the Green Tulip folded and died.

I remember one week, near the end of my tenure at the Plaza, when I myself became the object of some attention. The great comic actor Peter Sellers was in town, probably promoting a film, though I don't think he was staying on the premises. I was approached several times and asked if I were he. I even had a few requests for autographs. I was tempted, but I demurred. I could never see the resemblance, then or now, but it was a fitting celebrity moment, a finale of sorts, to my anomalous sojourn at "the world's most famous hotel."

The Other Cathedral
in Manhattan

For several years I lived a block away from the largest Gothic cathedral in the world. It wasn't in Chartres or Seville, nor Cologne or Canterbury. My city was New York, and the cathedral was St. John the Divine, on the Upper West Side of Manhattan.

When I was accepted at Columbia in 1963 to attend graduate school, I had no idea the neighborhood I'd be moving to contained not just one but two major houses of worship. A few blocks from the campus on Morningside Heights rises the impressive neo-Gothic Riverside Church, an interfaith bastion of liberal Christian activism. No slouch in the department of impressive statistics, Riverside is the tallest church in the United States.

But if you like your churches really big and really fancy, nothing compares to St. John the Divine. The day I first walked up its broad steps and into the nave I actually thought I was entering a massive Catholic cathedral. Who knew about high Episcopal and Protestant services with incense and bells and robed priests (albeit the marrying kind)?

I happened to wander in that particular afternoon during an evensong service. The sight of a few priests in black milling around and the sound of a choir singing down near the high altar a couple of football fields away did not dissuade me from assuming I was in Roman Catholic New York's holy of holies. But wasn't that actually St. Patrick's, which I had shuffled through several times on childhood holiday excursions to Radio City Music Hall?

I believe my confusion and false assumption that afternoon only added to my strong reaction of surprise, even stunned amazement. Although I was in a house of worship admittedly alien to me (a lapsed, if ever, practicing Presbyterian), I had stumbled into a place of great beauty and peace. What accounted for the kind of belief that could have created such a magnificent structure?

As many hours as I've spent in the ensuing years wandering up and down the five aisles of the nave of St. John's, sitting in one of the many small chapels, or attending any number of public events, both solemn and joyous, I've always remembered my initial impression that late fall afternoon.

I was never moved to consider becoming involved religiously; I was simply a great admirer of the cathedral as a place of solace and beauty. But I came to understand fully its impact on the believers: the stained glass windows, the flying buttresses, the lavish high altars, and the nave that extends for hundreds of feet and soars as if to the heavens. Whatever your faith or lack thereof, there's a degree of power and glory in cathedrals that you feel in few other places.

As it happened, I stayed on in New York and in the Columbia neighborhood after graduating, so my proximity to St. John's continued. From my last high-rise apartment in the late 1970s, I was able to look out my living room and bedroom windows across Broadway at the twin Gothic bell towers (still unfinished) of the great cathedral. I even had a steamy view from a small window in my bathroom shower.

In earlier years, I'd lived even closer, on a side street near Amsterdam Avenue. St. John's rises relatively close to the sidewalk on the east side of Amsterdam, in what was at that time an evolving neighborhood of small storefront establishments—a grocery/bodega, shoe repair shop, dry cleaner, and a hodgepodge of small restaurants ranging from pizza shops to my favorite, a Hungarian place called the Green Tree.

My ground-floor apartment was directly across the street from an old but active firehouse. The resident dalmatian, an old fellow, frequently drowsed away sunny afternoons on a mat in front of the station. I became virtually immune to the frequent wailing of sirens as red engines sped away into the night, but I always heard the pealing of the Schulmerich electronic bells that boomed from speakers in the unfinished towers of the cathedral.

I'd often leave work at Butler Library in time to walk over to the evensong service. I'd usually sit in the back of the nave and let the drone of the priest and the music of the youth choir relax and lull me as I gazed at the massive pillars, the elaborate high altar off in the distance, and the dusty play of the waning late afternoon light far up near the rafters.

I became familiar with the faces of several of the regular worshipers, though I don't recall that we ever talked or even acknowledged each other. They and I were in our own particular worlds; smiles, much less conversation, somehow seemed out of place.

I always felt blissfully alone on these occasions, even when a row of tour buses along Amsterdam Avenue warned me that throngs had descended. The cathedral is so immense that it swallows up visitors, even on the busiest and most festive days. When I left, I always gazed upward at the circular rose pattern of one of the world's most spectacular stained glass windows. On a nice afternoon, the hundreds of panels would blaze from the light of the sun setting over the Hudson River a few blocks to the west.

On days when I didn't go home for lunch (I could see the library from my kitchen window), I'd sometimes grab a sandwich at the deli or a falafel or two from a Mid-Eastern hole-in-the-wall on Broadway and head over to the cathedral grounds. The close consists of 13 acres, containing the bishop's residence, a private elementary school, smaller administrative buildings, a good-sized synod (meeting house), and carefully-tended gardens.

If I hadn't brought a book with me (often a pristine, still-uncatalogued library item I'd been waiting for), I'd watch the uniformed school kids at play, as well as passersby, including the several resident peacocks. I remember three of them were named Luke, Martha, and Matthew. The peacocks occasionally deigned to spread their magnificent feathers in my direction as they toddled past. (Graceful on foot they are not. As Oscar Wilde once said of a lady he didn't care for, "She is a peacock in everything but beauty."). In repose, however, the birds were spectacular.

The cathedral became part of the fabric of my life. In 1973 I attended a public service of remembrance for W. H. Auden, who lived on St. Mark's Place in the Village and had died a few weeks earlier in Vienna. Poets Galway Kinnell, Robert Penn Warren, and Muriel Ruykeyser offered tributes, and Psalm 130 was read ("Out of the depths I cry to you, O Lord..."). This lyric of despair was an apt choice, as Auden, a lifelong Anglican, had earlier contributed an appreciation to an edition of Oscar Wilde's essay of the same name written while he (Wilde) was serving hard labor in an English prison for "unnatural acts."

In 1974, 12,000 people packed the cathedral for the funeral of Duke Ellington. Overflow crowds filled the steps, the sidewalk, and the street. I was lucky to be there early enough to get inside. For me, the most moving part of the service was Ella Fitzgerald's renditions of Ellington's "In My Solitude" and the traditional hymn, "Just a Closer Walk with Thee," both sung with minimal accompaniment. The sound of her perfect voice in the pin-drop silence was unforgettable. It was a sublime moment.

Many New Yorkers associate St. John the Divine with the Paul Winter Consort. Winter has performed regularly at summer and winter solstice events ranging from simple, barely lit, no-sound-enhancement concerts to increasingly elaborate spectacles involving fancy technology and, for example, a huge "sun" gong that slowly rises into the upper reaches of the nave. If you haven't howled along with the recorded keening of a wolf, the sound reverberating throughout the vast expanse of St. John's, then you've missed an eerily beautiful, chill-inducing experience.

I'd left New York by 1984, but I drove down from Connecticut that fall to be present at the dedication of the Poets [Writers] Corner, tucked away in the north part of the cathedral. I went because the first inductees were Emily Dickinson and Walt Whitman. Washington Irving had also been unofficially selected earlier in the year, so the evening was a tribute to these three American writers.

I still have my program from this event. Walter Cronkite was the master of ceremonies, with readings by the Dean of the cathedral, actor Gregory Peck, and, again, Robert Penn Warren. Poet Edgar Bowers spoke for Emily Dickinson. The interior was lit with hundreds of candles, and the music was glorious (Bach, Gounod, Barber, and Schubert). I was happy to learn that night that Dickinson had received 12 of 13 votes on the first ballot cast by a panel of eminent American writers. Whitman and Melville vied for the second spot.

My times at St. John the Divine have become fewer in recent years, though whenever I see it again it's like meeting up with an old and dear companion. Five minutes into the visit, things are as they were. A couple of years ago, I spent the weekend in New York with a Connecticut friend. I wanted to show him my old stomping grounds, so we toured the Columbia campus, walked past several of my old apartment buildings, and ended up at the cathedral.

Matthew, Luke, and Martha now fan their feathers in peacock heaven, but there were new birds, including a completely white male whose plumage opened like a delicate, lacy mantilla. A huge statue called the "Peace Fountain" (no water in sight) sits in the garden these days. It's an eclectic grouping: the Archangel Michael, a decapitated Satan, a giant crab, the sun, the moon, seven giraffes, and a lion and lamb, all presumably representing the triumph of peace in the natural world. It's...uh...an attention-getter.

My friend and I walked inside and then down the long nave, amidst the "oohs" and "aahs" of the tourists (for the Rose Window, I presume). There are now more than 30 immortals memorialized in the Poets Corner, each identified by a plaque with an inscription from the writer's work. Walt Whitman's reads, "I stop somewhere waiting for you." Next to W.H. Auden are the lines, "If equal affection cannot be, let the more loving one be me." And under Emily Dickinson's name are the last two lines of her poem, "No rack can torture me": "Captivity is consciousness/So's liberty."

Dickinson's inner life and her art set her free. So, too, do I always feel joy and inspiration in the presence of this magnificent cathedral, whether on a visit or in remembered contemplation. In what Wordsworth calls "that inner eye that is the bliss of solitude," it's never far from my sight.

Hot Town

I

Summer in the City: Taking in a couple of foreign films at the funky Thalia Theater on Broadway and 95th, then walking home in the sultry night to my apartment on Morningside Heights, stopping on the way to buy fruit at the nearly-always-open outdoor stall on the corner of 110th...

...Picnicking on a sunny Sunday afternoon in nearby Riverside Park, checking out the passing joggers in their skimpy shorts and the summer students playing catch with orange and lime-green frisbees, sailboats gliding up the Hudson, and an occasional plane glinting high above in the cloudless sky...

...Descending into the concrete steaminess of the subway station platform, hotter than the street above, and then wedging into the briefly open door of a graffiti-covered car, hotter still, especially at rush hour when I squirm against the damp back of someone I've never seen before and may never see again...

...Riding my apartment elevator to the top floor and stepping onto tar beach, where I lounge on a folding chair next to the water tower...transistor radio, Tab, and magazines within easy reach, the Columbia campus spread out 12 floors below and the Empire State shimmering in the gauzy haze 80 blocks to the south...

II

I welcomed summer in the city. I hardly minded even the dog days of August, when the heat rose in visible waves from the sidewalk, and trash put out by the curb at dawn began to smell by 8 am.

In later years, long after I'd left New York for semi-rural eastern Connecticut, I began to avoid the blazing sun, and I grew to dislike even the slightest discomfort of a hot and clammy day. But this was not the case back then, when I loved being outdoors and experiencing New York weather in all its muggy glory.

In the late 60s and early 70s, I spent frequent weekends at the beach, usually one-day jaunts but occasionally a stay-over through Sunday. I had friends who had friends who had a cottage at the Pines, a predominantly gay enclave on Fire Island, a narrow stretch off the western end of Long Island. Another summer, I vacationed several weekends at the more conservative community of Fair Harbor, also on Fire Island, with a friend who had a share in a multi-bedroom house.

Most of my beach time, however, was spent at Riis Park. Named in honor of Jacob Riis, a turn-of–the-19th century New York social reformer, the beach is situated in

Rockaway, Queens, on a long barrier sandbar just south of Brooklyn.

After a long subway ride to Flatbush Avenue, last stop on the IRT#2 train, I'd board a bus for the refreshing drive across the flatlands and the long Marine Parkway Bridge. Arriving at Riis, we'd ride past the 5,000-car parking lot and be deposited directly in front of the immense Art Deco bathhouse. This imposing building was constructed during the Depression by Robert Moses, czar of 20th-century New York urban planning. Moses had stated that the park was to be "The People's Park," a haven reachable by public transportation, unlike the fancier Jones Beach further to the east.

A quick change, and off I'd trek to the gay and lesbian sections at the far end of the mile-long stretch of sand, past the largest area, mostly white, then through the Latino and black stretches, smaller but more densely populated and filled with the sounds of local radio stations blasting out soul and salsa tunes. I'd say these divisions were mostly the result of self-segregation; there was some mixing in all areas.

I wonder what Jacob Riis himself would have thought of this particular demographic pattern, emblematic of the late 20th century? Riis' best-known work was a photo-journalism exposé called *How the Other Half Lives*, but his subject was the tenements and factories of the Lower East Side, populated by mostly European immigrants.

What also set the gay and lesbian sections apart was the fact that they had gradually morphed over several summers into "clothing optional" beaches. What had begun with a few swimmers tying their bathing suits around their neck while in the water became full-fledged nudity. Initially, metropolitan police would occasionally patrol the area, resulting in some quick dressing or adjusting of towels and possibly a few arrests, but that gradually diminished by the late 1960s. In 1972, the National Park Service took over management of the beach and, apparently because of a lack of specific federal regulations, nudity seemed to be ignored, at least by the authorities.

Finding space in the gay section after a late morning arrival could be difficult, but I'd eventually spread out a blanket or come upon some early-risen friends who'd staked out a choice spot near the water, away from the twisty path over hot sand that led to the snack bar. Slipping off my trunks (oh yes, I did), I'd tune my radio to the common station being listened to by nearby blanket neighbors, most likely Jack Spector on WMCA or Cousin Brucie and Dan Ingram on WABC.

The two songs I remember most from those afternoons at Riis are The Supremes' "You Can't Hurry Love" and "Summer in the City" by The Lovin' Spoonful. Both tunes seemed to reverberate in the salt-tinged air for weeks during the summer of 1966.

Not everyone on the gay beach let it all hang out, but there was enough bare skin to make it somewhat notorious as a destination spot for those wanting to participate or gawk. Nudity back in those days was rare in films and on the stage, and the Internet was years in the future, so being surrounded by hundreds of naked men and a few women—close-up and in the flesh, as it were—had a certain appeal.

For me, the novelty always wore off after an hour, but it was still somewhat...disconcerting to open my eyes after a brief doze to the vertical-angle sight of a "partially tanned" swimmer swinging by, inches away, after a frolic in the water. Mostly, however, so many bare bodies became just that, and it was only the exceptional specimen—or the beach-goer you wished had kept it all on—who attracted notice.

Ironically, the people I seem to remember most vividly at Riis were not those displaying their wares but another group of regulars, the folks at the Neponsit Nursing Home, situated directly behind the beach. These elderly residents, men and women alike, would meander down over the course of the afternoon to the chain-link fence that separated the facility from the park. They'd stand watching, sometimes waving to no one in particular, though who knows? Others remained further back, relaxing on chairs as they took in what must have been a scene they'd never have imagined experiencing at this point in their lives, certainly not one touted, I'd imagine, in Neponsit marketing brochures.

Despite the potential for raucous behavior, I witnessed only a few instances of sexual shenanigans on the blankets, and those rather discreetly conducted. I suspect there was more going on in the water; perhaps not. There was the occasional police presence to be mindful of, though they rarely strolled down from the boardwalk. Whatever...Heat, sand, and slathered Coppertone, to my mind, do not make for an ambiance conducive to hanky-panky.

III

An afternoon at Riis Park might be capped off in the evening by another activity, this of a more cultural nature. Summer in the city also meant outdoor concerts and plays. The Rheingold (later, Schaefer) Central Park Music Festival, Shakespeare in the Park, and concerts at City College's Lewisohn Stadium all provided a trove of entertainment ranging from folk singers to the Bard to grand opera.

I didn't attend many Shakespeare in the Park performances during my years in New York, and I regret that. It always seemed a hassle to wait in line to get a ticket (they were free on a first-come, first-served basis), and so I usually passed. What was I thinking?

I did see James Earl Jones as a commanding Othello back in 1964, but the production that stays with me was 14 years later, when I was invited by a friend who'd been given tickets in advance to *The Taming of the Shrew*. I remember that evening well. The leads were the late, lamented Raúl Juliá, memorable a couple of years earlier as Macheath in *Threepenny Opera* at Lincoln Center, and Meryl Streep, then at the beginning of her spectacular career. The night was beautiful and the bugs stayed home. Juliá and especially, Streep, made me understand Shakespearean language as never before.

Central Park figured in many of my other summer nights as well. For several years in the late 60s and early 70s, the Schaefer Brewing Company sponsored a music festival in the Wollman Skating Rink at the southern end of the park, just off Central Park South. Though ticket lines formed early in the day, I always bought mine at an outlet at the old Korvette's department store over on Fifth Avenue. Unbelievably, they cost all of one dollar, rising, I think, to three by 1975.

I saw an impressive array of singers here, ranging from Judy Collins, Arlo Guthrie, and Melanie (This was the 60s!) to Nina Simone, the incomparable Ella Fitzgerald, and Peggy Lee, who played the festival several times.

Lee, in particular, made a lasting impression on me. She was a compelling performer, and I recall one balmy, breezy evening when she arrived on stage in a flowing, nearly diaphanous white gown and began the program with a song she wrote, "I Love Being Here with You." As the concert progressed and twilight came, the nearby trees and skyscrapers were framed against the sky, as were the outlines of non-ticket holders who'd climbed onto the big rocks surrounding the rink. The acoustics were superb, and Lee's voice, husky and knowing, floated seductively over the enthralled, hushed crowd.

Singers of a different sort were featured at another outdoor venue I frequented in my very early years in the big city: Lewisohn Stadium, north of Columbia on the campus of City College. A victim of the wrecking ball in 1983, the stadium was designed as a classical amphitheater. For several summers it hosted performers from the Metropolitan Opera, as well as other classical artists, big names like Van Cliburn.

I was introduced to live opera at Lewisohn in the summer of 1965 by a good friend I'd met when I'd arrived at Columbia two years earlier. My only previous exposure had been when I'd watched famous opera stars singing brief arias on TV on the Sunday night Ed Sullivan Show, sandwiched between acts like Señor Wences and Bo Diddley. That summer I saw, in concert versions and for one dollar each, Regina Resnik in *Carmen*, Jan Peerce and Roberta Peters in *Rigoletto*, and Dorothy Kirsten and Richard Tucker in *Tosca*.

That summer, too, I had the great good luck to hear two renowned divas, then in the later stages of their careers. Renata Tebaldi, still formidable though a few years from a somewhat early retirement, performed solo in an opening season concert to a sold-out crowd of 8,000. And the legendary Zinka Milanov, of whom composer Virgil Thompson wrote, "She sings with a beauty unmatched among the sopranos of this country," performed at Lewisohn a few weeks later. Milanov, then nearly 60, sang Puccini's "O Mio Babbino Caro" as an encore to a thunderously appreciative audience. Later, my more knowledgeable friends debated which of the two singers (Tebaldi had done the same aria) performed it better. After heated debate, no consensus was reached. To me, both were sublime.

I can't profess to ever becoming an opera fanatic, though over the years I saw my share, both at the Met and the New York City Opera. But whenever I hear "O Mio Babbino Caro," I think of Milanov, and the beautiful notes that wafted softly through the night air of the majestic amphitheater.

On the other hand, whenever the opening bars of "You Can't Hurry Love" hit the airwaves on a golden oldies radio station, I turn up the volume and my mind races back to that hot summer on the beach at Riis Park.

Which of these memories is the more visceral? It's hard to say.

Vanished in Manhattan

The small, independent bookstore in American cities and towns just about disappeared from the landscape when Barnes & Noble and Borders began to stake their claims in malls from Hyannis to Honolulu. Now I grieve the absence of even these behemoths, themselves the victims of online retailers, who have—virtually, as it were—wiped these brick-and-mortar superstores pretty much off the map.

The bookstores that were a big part of my life in New York for nearly two decades are now mostly gone, vanished for a variety of reasons: the death of a longtime owner, prohibitive monthly rents, the real estate wrecking ball, competition from discount chains, and, most probably, the altered buying patterns of a public increasingly more interested in easy sound-bytes than challenging reading.

Back in the day (we're talking 1960s-1970s), there was a wide variety of bookstores to which I regularly made the rounds, some in my Upper West Side neighborhood, others in the Village, and a few in the more expensive mid-town area, where bargain titles were readily available at the ubiquitous

Marboro stores. Marboro books were "remaindered," meaning they'd been purchased in lots to be sold at steeply discounted prices—the end of the line as far as the book's in-print retail life.

In my early years as a grad student at Columbia, I frequented Salter's Books. Salter's was a storefront shop located diagonally across from the main entrance to the campus, next to the always busy Chock Full o'Nuts coffee house on the corner of 116th Street.

Salter's had frequent sidewalk sales, perhaps as a last-ditch effort to make more space in its incredibly cramped quarters. Inside, there was an attempt at organization and classification of the thousands of volumes on display, including course texts, but there was little concern for neatness and tidy aisles. I had the impression that the stools, stacks of books, and worksheets scattered everywhere were evidence that inventory and shelf tasks, however valiantly begun, were interrupted by more pressing activities—helping a customer, perusing a new title or two, breaking for coffee—and never resumed to completion.

A grad school acquaintance, Joe, worked scattered hours at Salter's, and I'd often show up, a paper cup of that "heavenly" coffee from next door in hand, on the likely chance he'd be free to talk. I didn't really buy books at Salter's, other than the odd required text, but I spent a lot of time there.

My modest book purchases in those days consisted mostly of the cheapest titles I could find, and the Manhattan of 40 or 50 years ago had plenty of stores with equally modest prices.

For rock-bottom buys, those Marboro stores, in locations all over the city, couldn't be bettered. I often wondered how an author would react to seeing stacks of his books—a telltale colored marker slash across the top edge—on tables labeled with "$1 CLOSEOUT" signs. Would the writer feel embarrassment? Grief? Anger? Having since experienced the vicissitudes of the book trade, I now tend to view remainders as an indication that the titles at least made it through the publication process, however overly optimistic the publisher may have been. Former bestsellers eventually ended up on the remainder tables, too, but at slightly higher prices.

For fancier books (photograph collections, art reproductions, and others of the coffee table ilk), Barnes & Noble and Strand were the places to go. Before B&N expanded to retail outlets throughout Manhattan and eventually the entire country, they operated out of a huge building on lower Fifth Avenue. This was the store I roamed through for hours at a time, especially the upper floors, where deeply discounted sale items were displayed neatly on endless shelves and along seeming miles of aisles of carefully arranged bins. I still have a few of the books purchased on Saturday excursions to that store, carted on the subway to whatever Upper West Side apartment I was living in at the time.

Strand, located south of Barnes & Noble on 12th Street and Broadway, was, or seemed to be, even larger. Strand was more in keeping with the Salter school of marketing and display: Though the stock was organized—sort of—the place was jammed with books, both shelved and piled. There were knowledgeable clerks—many clerks—and, of course, always a mob of book lovers crowding the narrow aisles and browsing the overflowing bins. Strand, now a legend in the American book trade, is the only bookstore I frequented that still exists today as it was then: same location, same crowded aisles, still the place to go to experience a couple of hours of book-browsing heaven.

Farther east was the legendary Booksellers Row, a strip along Fourth Avenue that in its heyday housed well over 25 bookstores, most of them small, dingy storefronts staffed by the owner and open irregular hours. These bookstores were not in a location I regularly passed through or otherwise frequented, so a trip to the Row was a foray into a funkier, more borderline neighborhood than the surrounding Village area. Fourth Avenue is the southern extension of Park Avenue, but in those days it was far removed in every other way from that rarefied thoroughfare. The Bowery, at that time still very much the last, bleak, sad refuge of the dispossessed and downtrodden, was just a few blocks to the south.

I didn't regularly frequent Booksellers Row, except for an occasional search for a particular title, such as an out-of-print copy of a travel volume by the great and remarkably prolific English writer, H. V. Morton. (I'd discovered him at a bookstore in London's Cecil Court, a magical street of booksellers straight out of the Victorian past between Charing Cross Road and St. Martin's Lane, but that's another chapter of my book-browsing memories.) I also once found an early 1890s edition of Emily Dickinson along Booksellers Row, at Dauber & Pine, Peter Stammer's, or the Abbey, I don't remember which. These worthy shops are all gone now.

Vanished, too, are the specialty shops, such as Murder Ink, on the upper West Side. When on the lam from whatever graduate term paper was pursuing me at the time, I liked to peruse the latest books at this cozy store by relatively new writers such as Tony Hillerman and P. D. James. And I still have a big poster reproduction of silent film star Douglas Fairbanks riding his magic carpet in *The Thief of Baghdad* that I bought at the New Yorker Bookstore, around the corner from the venerable Broadway movie theater of the same name.

Down in Greenwich Village I liked the tiny Oscar Wilde Bookstore, initially at its Mercer Street location and later over on Christopher, appropriately near the Stonewall Bar, historic site of the gay uprising in the summer of 1969. The Oscar Wilde hung on for many years, finally succumbing in 2009 to rent increases, online buying options, and the mainstreaming of gay literature into the popular culture and, consequently, into the stock of the bigger chains.

The Phoenix on tiny Jones Street was another store I occasionally visited, and I had a brief acquaintance with Robert A. Wilson, the owner, an erudite and serious book collector and bibliographer whose illustrious friends included W. H. Auden and Alan Ginsberg. I was happy to discover not long ago Bob Wilson's 2001 memoir *Seeing Shelley Plain*, wherein he recounts in gracefully written detail his adventures in the Manhattan book trade.

The Eighth Street Bookshop was another of my obligatory stops. These frequent forays might also include visits to Sutter's Bakery over near Sheridan Square or dimly lit Village coffee houses like the Figaro on Bleecker or, perhaps later in the day, attendance at folk music performances at the Village Gate or foreign and independent films at the Bleecker Street Cinema.

The Eighth Street Bookshop was, more than any other New York bookstore, the center of the East Coast Beat movement of the Fifties and early Sixties, and it had remained a welcoming literary beacon in the days I roamed the Village. Eighth Street in the 1970s was still one of *the* Village streets, always teeming with pedestrians on the weekend. The shop's three floors of books attracted a constant stream of customers from the narrow street—Villagers and other New Yorkers, tourists, kids from the suburbs spending a day in town. I suppose there were some serious buyers, but most of us were indefatigable window-shoppers. I only occasionally actually bought a book at the Eighth Street. Bookshop browsing—again, the operative phrase—remains a vivid and fond memory of my two decades of life in the big city.

Though most of the bookstores of my time in New York are gone, many of the books I bought remain with me, a few in my bedroom, some in my den, most in makeshift shelves in my basement waiting to be opened once again. I like what Nicholson Baker, novelist, essayist, passionate bibliophile, and fierce advocate of paper-based media, once wrote: "Printed books usually outlive bookstores and the publishers who brought them out. They sit around, demanding nothing for decades. That's one of their nicest qualities—their brute persistence."

Bus Ride to the Middle Ages

These days I love nothing better than taking an occasional trip from Connecticut to the big city. But at the end of a Saturday spent in Manhattan—dodging traffic, walking zig-zag to avoid distracted or fast-paced pedestrians, steeling my ears against the incessant honks and squealing of brakes, and generally upping the speed and intensity of my every thought and action—I wonder how I spent the greater part of 20 years living amid this pandemonium.

I was young, yes, and I couldn't get enough of what New York had to offer, and in time I probably got used to navigating my own path through the frenzied landscape that surrounded me. But I also discovered, fairly early on, places in Manhattan that offered a respite from the mad pace and incessant buzz of life in the city.

One of these oases was the Cloisters, perched in northern Manhattan at the highest point on the island.

A branch of the Metropolitan Museum of Art, the Cloisters sits at the far end of Fort Tryon Park, itself a 67-acre haven of leafy tranquility. The land was bought and developed in the early twentieth century by John D. Rockefeller Jr. as a site to display, in a bucolic setting, his collection of medieval art. The park and museum rise on the heights of the east bank of the Hudson, across from the cliffs of the New Jersey Palisades. In spirit a million miles from Times Square, this replica of a medieval sanctuary is in fact only a 30-minute subway ride away.

I preferred to catch the #4 bus on Broadway as it heads north to Fort Washington Avenue, terminating its route at the entrance to Fort Tryon Park. Like the immense suspension bridge spanning the river nearby, this avenue that leads to the park is named for you-know-who, that revered American Father who apparently managed (when he wasn't leading the troops or sleeping hither and yon) to be here, there, and everywhere during the years of the Revolution.

Another ubiquitous name in our cultural history, that of prolific landscape architect Frederick Law Olmstead, figures prominently in the area's heritage: Olmstead's son, Frederick Jr., designed the 66 acres of Fort Tryon Park, a more modest effort than his father's massive Central Park, 80 blocks south.

Sometimes I'd pause on my way through Fort Tryon Park, especially in midsummer when the heather garden was in full flower. I was always reminded of my grandmother and the masses of purple shrubs growing on the hills bordering the farm she grew up on in the far north of Scotland.

Usually, however, I'd head straight through the park to the museum's entrance. On a damp or windy day, I'd spend most of my time inside. With inclement weather, I could be relatively certain that I'd have several of the exhibit rooms to myself, and even on sunny weekends, at least during the decades of the 60s and 70s, it wasn't hard to elude the modest number of visitors who'd ventured beyond the usual "must see" tourist spots in Midtown.

I always stopped off in one gallery to visit the beautiful unicorn tapestries. Several panels relate, in startlingly vivid color, the sad, religiously allegorical tale of the hunt and capture of this mythical beast. The room was always occupied by visitors who had clearly made the trek to see the building's most celebrated treasure.

But I really preferred solitude, and so I'd seek out one of the smaller chambers. There was one in particular, a small but high-ceiling chapel, that was often unoccupied. Seated on a small wooden chair, I liked to rest, mind and body alike, and imagine myself back in medieval times. Knowing that the room was constructed of stones assembled from several European religious sites in France and Spain helped in transporting me back to another time and place. There was total silence and tranquility in this small chapel, the muted sky of a cloudy afternoon only partially lighting the hushed interior. I felt myself in the cloistered quarters of a centuries-old monastery.

On warm and sunny days, however, there was no lovelier place to stroll than outdoors in the gardens, several encircled by arched passageways. Sometimes I'd just lean against one of the stone walls that overlook the majestic Hudson. Here, I imagined the ghosts of monks—perhaps Catalans who'd followed their familiar surroundings being shipped across the Atlantic—puttering about as they tended their herbs and vegetables.

I seemed, in those moments, to be part of two worlds. Lost in a medieval reverie, I'd gaze at the silver steel cables of the George Washington Bridge glittering not far to the south. Further downriver, had it been evening, I'd have been able to see the lights on the Jersey side of the old Palisades Amusement Park, still going strong in the late 1960s.

Way to the south, the towers of mid-Manhattan rose, shimmering delicately in the sunlight like a futuristic mirage of what was to come a few centuries hence. Occasionally a speedboat cut a white wake in the river below, a far remove from the Dutch sails of the Half-Moon that carried explorer Henry Hudson slowly up the river in 1609.

By the time I finished my return stroll through Fort Tryon Park, past the hot dog vendor and jewelry seller and would-be Dylan balladeer, I'd transitioned back to the 20th century. Enjoying a giant hot pretzel before boarding the downtown bus might feed my late afternoon hunger; my mind and soul were already well-replenished.

1001 Nights at The
New York City Ballet

Along with seeing every Broadway and Off-Broadway show I could afford, I also became a certified balletomane during my early years in New York. Though I sampled just about every kind of dance performance—from the religious ecstasy of the Whirling Dervishes to the angular writing of Martha Graham—I soon gravitated toward classical ballet.

On the surface, ballet is the most poised and disciplined form of dance. With the greatest of ballet artists, however, the display of remarkable grace within formal patterns also reflects the tension between technical control and inner passion. This pull is kept in check, but with the most exciting dancers it often teeters on the brink of reckless abandonment.

What sparked my love of this rarefied form of dance? It was certainly a kind of movement I couldn't hope to emulate myself (you didn't see many graceful jumps and spins at most of the '70s discos and bars I patronized). I'd been a wallflower on the high school dance floor, and I was also on the low end of the skating skills scale. I could barely stand on blades, and I never mastered the art of stopping when attached to a pair of rapidly moving roller skates.

The closest I'd come to seeing ballet was the classic British film *The Red Shoes*, a gaudy, melodramatic story of a dancer with who comes to an ill-fated demise. It was all a bit over my head, though I remember enjoying the morbid spectacle of the ballerina feverishly dancing herself to death on those treacherous toe shoes.

But in the spring of 1962, when I was a junior at Brown, the old Ballet Russe de Monte Carlo performed in Providence at the Veterans Memorial Auditorium, a venerable, ornately appointed theater on a rise near the State Capitol. My friend Myron and I decided to venture down College Hill and buy a couple of cheap tickets.

Most of the program is a vague memory, but I vividly recall the major piece, *Scheherazade*, set to Rimsky-Korsakov's lushly romantic score and choreographed by the great Michel Fokine, who was closely associated with the Ballet Russe in its early days in Europe. The music was wonderful and, from my upper balcony seat, the stage glittered in shades of gold and red. What completely enthralled me was the bravura dancing of the Sultan's concubine and her forbidden lover (a role originated by the legendary Nijinsky) as they played out their tragic Arabian Nights story.

Although I eventually came to prefer the more abstract ballets of George Balanchine, I was overwhelmed that night by the movement, the exotic music, and the sets and costumes of this renowned touring company. I knew for sure I'd be seeing more ballet at some point in the future.

The following year, I found myself in grad school at Columbia, immersed in academic life on Morningside Heights. But I did manage to take in a lot of night life, and from the moment I attended my first performance of the New York City Ballet (NYCB) in the fall of 1963, I was hooked.

Lincoln Center was under construction at that time, near the neighborhood where the opening dance scenes of the movie *West Side Story* had been filmed a few years earlier. The NYCB was still holding court over on West 55th Street at City Center. Tickets for the rear balcony of this cavernous Moorish Revival theater were 95 cents, but for most performances I was able to scoot downstairs after the first intermission and claim a choice orchestra seat for the remaining dances.

I can't count the number of nights I spent sitting in the dark at City Center that first year in New York, discovering all the George Balanchine—as well as the early Jerome Robbins—ballets. The tuning of the orchestra strings, the dimming of the enormous Arabesque chandeliers, the brisk arrival of conductor Robert Irving, the opening of the massive red curtain...and I was off on another magical trip to the land where everyone spoke the same two languages: music and dance. As Balanchine once said of the orchestra under Irving's baton, "If you don't like what you're watching, close your eyes and enjoy the great concert."

In later years, I occasionally had two concurrent subscriptions to City Ballet, in addition to single tickets to various performances by great international companies— the Bolshoi, British Royal Ballet, Stuttgart, and the National Ballet of Cuba. In decent weather I'd hike the couple of miles from wherever on the Upper West Side I happened to be living. When you're a New Yorker, walking becomes part of your daily routine. If I was tired after the performance (but who's ever really tired when you're young and living in Manhattan?), I'd hop on the local uptown IRT for the ten-minute subway ride home.

There were many greats at NYCB whose careers overlapped with my time in New York: Jacques D'Amboise, Patricia McBride, Edward Villella, Gelsey Kirkland, and Peter Martins. I wasn't a "ballet groupie," but I did have a favorite dancer, Suzanne Farrell, who epitomized for me that hallmark combination of discipline, flawless technique, and an almost heedless intensity. You rarely watched anyone else when Farrell was on stage; she was a thrilling dancer. Often described as the greatest ballerina of the 20th century, she was probably supreme among Balanchine's many muses over the course of his long creative career.

I also got a chance to see and meet young Balanchine dancers in training when I taught high school English at the Professional Children's School on West 60th Street, just south of Lincoln Center. Several landed contracts with major companies, including the NYCB, and I followed their careers long after I left New York. Others—musicians, actors, ice skaters—became well known as well, but that's a story for another chapter.

I soon grew to prefer Balanchine's mostly minimalist, abstract works to the full-length "story" ballets (think *Coppélia* and *Sleeping Beauty*) that other companies generally favored. Balanchine had a long partnership with Igor Stravinsky, who composed several pieces for him, perhaps most notably the majestic *Agon*. There is no set, no apparent story, no "tuneful" melodies. The 12 dancers wear plain black and white rehearsal costumes as they dance in a series of intricate patterns and pairings, including a long pas de deux that is both formal in technique and sensual in its intimacy. If you could hold your breath during this 25-minute masterpiece, you would.

My favorite Balanchine ballet is probably *Chaconne*, because of the beautiful Gluck music (from *Orfeo ed Euridice*) as well as the return to the company of Suzanne Farrell after a hiatus of several years in Europe. Balanchine created this ballet for her, and I saw its premiere on January 22, 1976, a landmark event for diehard City Ballet fans.

I continued to haunt Lincoln Center throughout the '70s, enjoying new dancers and celebrating the careers of those who retired, usually around the age of 40. As is true with sports athletes, the dancer's life is a short one.

When I made the decision to move from New York back to New England, I had several concerns, not the least of them involving the cultural life I'd be leaving. I was acutely aware I'd be hard-pressed to find in rural Eastern Connecticut anything close to the arts mecca that was and is New York.

As it happened, I discovered that nearby Hartford and the various local college communities had much to offer in the way of theater, and I was happy to discover that the Hartford Ballet (now defunct) was more than good. And yet...It wasn't the New York City Ballet, nor did I expect it would be. That void never did get filled.

I continued over the years to follow the fortunes of the NYCB. Balanchine died in 1983, two years after I left the city, but other choreographers have emerged in recent years. One winter season I bought a subscription, but with weather interference, an inconvenient bout of the flu, and last-minute program changes, it didn't quite work out. I felt the NYCB slipping away.

In the past few years, however, I've managed to make the trip to Lincoln Center more than a few times, and I'm beginning to become familiar with a whole new crop of dancers. Every dancer I remember from my time in the city is retired, but the company is still probably the best there is. No other ballet organization comes close to the variety of works in its repertory, or the number of world-class dancers. Nevertheless, it's still a shock to see a program advertised as an "All Balanchine" evening. In my day, the company *was* Balanchine.

A few weeks ago I was riding home to Connecticut on a late Metro North train after spending a Saturday in the city. I'd visited the Metropolitan Museum, had lunch at a Malaysian restaurant near Lincoln Center, and attended an NYCB matinee at the David H. Koch Theater (formerly the New York State Theater) at Lincoln Center. It had been a wonderful day.

As the train made its familiar suburban stops— Greenwich, Darien, Westport—I found my mind drifting away from the pages of my *New Yorker* and back to the performance I'd seen earlier that afternoon. I'd picked a program that included pieces choreographed by Balanchine and Christopher Wheeldon, perhaps the most acclaimed contemporary ballet choreographer. The dancers were looking good, and I was happy to have seen two of my favorites, veterans Joaquin De Luz and Maria Kowroski, as well as several new (to me), impressive young dancers.

Wary of falling asleep and missing my stop—the train car doors always open and close within a few seconds at this late hour—I nevertheless reclined in my seat and thought back on my ballet-going days and my old life in Manhattan. Not for one moment am I truly sorry that I left more than three decades ago, but when you make a big decision, there are always trade-offs—that's part of why it's a big decision.

I'll always have regret that I can't, on the spur of the moment, lock my apartment door, stroll down Broadway to Lincoln Center, pick up a ballet ticket, watch the lights go down, and marvel at the magic unfolding before me.

Up against the Wall! Part II: Stonewall 1969

The late Sixties was a heady time to be living in any urban area with a large gay population. The Big Apple was no exception. Along with San Francisco, New York was a powerful magnet for those anywhere right of center on Dr. Alfred Kinsey's sexual scale. Unlike most of the rest of the country, still very much in thrall to the conformity of the Eisenhower Fifties, New York was the answer to many a young man's fantasies of life as it could be led.

In the summer of 1969, I'd been a New Yorker for six years. By day an English teacher at a private secondary school in midtown Manhattan, at night I was usually out on the town—at the theater, the ballet, or in one of the many bars in Greenwich Village.

I was living in a brownstone on the Upper West Side, on a quiet, tree-shaded block near Riverside Park and the Hudson. Through a happy coincidence, the eight small apartments were occupied mostly by a number of friends like me—young, single and gay. Typically for this area of

Manhattan, we were a mix of ethnicities—White, Black, Hispanic, and Asian.

On the hot and humid evening of Friday, June 27, 1969, we were having one of our frequent all-building parties, which usually started "officially" in one apartment, then drifted out into the hallway and stairs, and eventually occupied all four floors. These galas generally lasted into the wee hours, and you never knew just where you might end up by early morning.

Sometime after midnight, Javier, a grad student from Argentina who lived on the top floor, arrived home from Greenwich Village with big news. "There's a commotion down at the Stonewall," he told us. "Lots of police and people throwing stuff, and they've got the street blocked off."

We all knew the Stonewall, a bar on Christopher Street in the West Village, crummier than most, and run, like many gay bars, by the Mafia (with, apparently, some collusion from New York's Finest). Watered-down drinks were one dollar (relatively expensive in those days), and the bathrooms tended to flood regularly. It was not an elegant place, but its seediness did not stop us from going back, again and again.

After hearing Javier's excited report on the goings-on, we contemplated abandoning our party and heading right down to the Village. But the hour was late, and, besides, it didn't sound like much more than a somewhat stronger reaction than usual to one of the police raids that occurred regularly at the Stonewall and elsewhere.

I'd been in bars that were raided many times. The usual scenario consisted of a short warning (lights flashing, someone shouting, "It's a raid!"), and the next thing you knew you were being herded, like slow-moving cattle, out onto Christopher Street. Sometimes you had to pass through a gauntlet of cops, a few looking fierce, others impassive, one or two embarrassed.

Occasionally, but not often, some patrons were marched into waiting paddy wagons, taken to the local precinct station, and then released. That particularly ignominy never happened to me. Mostly we dispersed into the street and headed off to another bar, or we waited for an hour or so and then returned to the scene of the crime after whatever arrangements had been made between management and the police. It was a game, somewhat humiliating, especially in retrospect, but one not without a certain sense of wacky adventurousness. You just went along with it; it was part of the deal.

This raid, however, proved to be different. Sometime the next day—Saturday, June 28, another hot one—a friend who lived near the bar phoned and told me that the demonstration had, in fact, lasted through the night and was picking up steam. "Come on down!" he urged.

By early evening some of us were sufficiently recovered and rested from the night before to pay our 20 cents subway fare and take the IRT local to Sheridan Square, a major crossroads in the West Village and a block away from the Stonewall. The train seemed to be especially crowded with gay men, not a particularly unusual occurrence on a Saturday night, though it was still way too early for the regular bar crowd.

As soon as we emerged onto Christopher and 7th Avenue, we found ourselves in the midst of a dense and noisy mob. Surprisingly, the street in front of the Stonewall was not blocked off to pedestrians or traffic, but it was impossible to do more than mill around the periphery. The bar seemed to be closed, and the windows were boarded up. Directly across the street, members of the New York Tactical Patrol Force (TPF) stood in formation, wearing helmets with visors and carrying batons and shields.

I was reminded of the Columbia student uprising a year earlier, but this scene, possibly because of the tighter space, seemed far louder, rowdier, and more flamboyant. There was also an added element of rage and potential violence that hadn't really erupted at Columbia until the eventual storming of the occupied buildings that finally ended that uprising.

Now I watched as demonstrators scrawled slogans like "SUPPORT GAY POWER" and "LEGALIZE GAY BARS" on the boarded-up window of the bar. Police tried to keep people away from the immediate vicinity, but crowds would retreat en masse down one end of the block and then soon reappear at the other. Any cars that attempted to enter Christopher Street were rocked and jumped on by the crowds of mostly young men. I saw the top of a parked police cruiser crushed by a concrete block dropped from an upper window.

Chaotic activity seemed to come in waves. Some of the local queens formed a sort of Rockettes chorus line and chanted, "We are the girls from Stonewall" until cops rushed at them, smashing their nightsticks against anything they could hit. Minutes later, the girls, undaunted, were back, and the same scenario unfolded again…and again.

From the tiny park adjacent to the square, onlookers hurled bottles, bricks, and other objects, many striking observers as well as the police. Trashcans were set on fire. Many men in the crowd were holding hands and kissing, something I'd never seen happen before on this scale in a public place.

Several participants in the previous night's events had shown up, a few of them conspicuous by their bandages and wounds. I remember one Puerto Rican kid, arm in a white sling and face completely swollen, bruised and scabbed.

"What did you do last night?" I asked him.

"Not a fuckin' thing. They just clubbed us. My friend's got a broken shoulder, and I heard some guy's in a coma over at Roosevelt."

Some of the Rockettes contingent posed for flash photographs and regaled the crowds with tales of what had happened the previous evening. Other demonstrators, sober and serious, distributed flyers that demanded, "GET THE MAFIA AND COPS OUT OF GAY BARS."

I saw several men whom I recognized from other nights at the Stonewall, many of them young, street-wise locals, others from the surrounding boroughs, along with the aforementioned drag queens who also frequented the bar. The boys and men in drag usually congregated in a smaller room off to the side, so those of us in the main bar area tended to mingle with them only on the dance floor. Still, this was one of the few places where I saw and occasionally talked to gay men whose sense of style resulted in outfits much more interesting than my and others' costume of jeans, tight tee shirt, and sneakers.

In those days, you rarely saw anyone in full drag in any bar, or even on the street, though there was an after-hours place called Washington Square, as well as Club 82 in the East Village, where cross-dressing was more prevalent. Stonewall catered to a mix of patrons, although more conservative, older gays tended to frequent other bars, like the legendary Julius', just around the corner, and the Candy Store, further uptown on 56th just off Fifth Avenue (ties and jackets were common attire here). Keller's and The Stud, both in the Village, attracted those who were into leather and other, more extreme exotica. Keller's displayed a magazine behind the bar called *Black and Blue*.

As I left Sheridan Square that night, I bought the Sunday *Times*, expensive at 50 cents but always eagerly awaited on Saturdays around 10 pm at subway newsstands throughout the city. On the ride uptown I looked for mention of the riot from the night before. Deep within the paper there was a short article with the headline "4 POLICEMEN HURT IN 'VILLAGE' RAID ...MELEE NEAR SHERIDAN SQUARE FOLLOWS ACTION AT BAR."

The report was brief, with no reference to previous raids, arrests, and nothing from the point of view of the protesters. That kind of minimal coverage would continue in the *Times* for the next several days, though the tabloid *Daily News* played it up with photos and longer pieces.

The next afternoon—Sunday—I went to the house of a friend in the Village for brunch. We decided to stroll over to the Stonewall, where the activity had continued on, ebbing early in the morning and then once again picking up as the third day began.

On the way, we stopped at Sutter's Bakery, long gone and lamented, for a cup of coffee and a piece of their incredible multi-layered French buttercream cake. Occupying the second floor of the building next to Sutter's was the tiny office of the young *Village Voice* newspaper, which did give much more extensive and serious coverage to Stonewall.

A block away from Sutter's stood the massive Women's House of Detention, a bizarre pink concrete edifice that always had a few bystanders standing at its base yelling up at the ladies in the windows. The inmates were more than happy to holler back. On this particular day, there was a lot of milling about and two-way conversation, and the subject was mostly Stonewall. I remember one woman shouting down from a high story window, "Anyone seen Sylvia over there?"

"Yeah, she's there," somebody in the crowd yelled.

"Then tell her Birdie says to get her fuckin' ass over to see me," bellowed the voice from the window. "Tell her to get herself arrested!"

As we arrived back at Sheridan Square, I was surprised at the activity still going on. Amazingly, the bar had reopened for business, and a steady stream of customers wandered in and out. But the police were there in full force, including several on horseback. I saw another damaged cruiser, this one with its front windshield shattered. A parking meter lay overturned in the street, and I later learned that it had actually been used on the first night to batter the entrance door to the bar.

I stood awhile, observing, too chicken to go in, and then left. We later found out the Tactical Patrol Force eventually cleared the immediate area. I also heard that Allen Ginsberg visited the bar in the evening, encouraging the patrons inside. In a later interview he described them as "...beautiful... they've lost that wounded look that fags all had ten years ago." Sporadic gatherings occurred over the next few days, but the demonstration was essentially over.

Did I realize that I'd been present at a seminal moment in American sociopolitical history? Perhaps not that weekend, though Stonewall was certainly the most dramatic example I'd personally witnessed in terms of a minority group taking a stand. I'm not sure it was the single event of Stonewall itself those few days, but rather its snowball effect over the following months that signaled the changes that were to come.

So much happened in 1969: King's killing, Robert Kennedy's murder, troop escalation to half a million men in Vietnam, the tumultuous Democratic Convention in Chicago, the moon walk, Woodstock—and the emergence or renewed efforts of many gay activist organizations, most notably the Gay Liberation Front. These were both awful and wonderful times, perhaps unparalleled in American history in terms of the short span in which history-changing events occurred.

In the months after Stonewall, I began to join in gay demonstrations around the city. I clearly remember marching on Fifth Avenue in those early days. Basically, we were a small group of people—men and women—simply walking in the street rather than on the sidewalk. There were no floats, no costumes, perhaps a few signs and banners. I was always very aware of the tourists gawking at us from the sidewalk, and I was never comfortable during those early peaceful protests. But I kept on marching.

Perhaps taking to the street occasionally wasn't such a big gesture on my part, but it probably wouldn't have happened at all had it not been for the brave protesters and demonstrators at Stonewall. Occurring in the midst of other social upheaval that pivotal year, this small uprising is now rightfully seen as a turning point in the gay civil rights movement. We'd all had enough.

Random Thoughts of a
Depressed New Yorker

A *ccording to the date I carefully noted on the carbon*
copy, I wrote this piece in March 1979, two years
before I left Manhattan. It must have been composed
in the aftermath of some big-city indignity I'd recently
experienced on the streets or elsewhere. Still, I'm surprised
and a bit taken aback at the vehemence and churlishness of
my attitude at the time.

Granted, New York in the late 70s was not the city of a
decade earlier. Though I had mixed feelings about relocating,
in most ways I was glad to be leaving for Connecticut. But
I don't remember the city being quite the cauldron of urban
angst I describe. These days, when I visit friends, I'm amazed
at the cleanliness, the complete overhaul of the subway
system, and the general sense of well-being and safety that
now characterizes the street scene in Manhattan.

I don't recall my goal, if any, in writing the piece, and
I don't know what became of the original. I don't believe
the essay was published anywhere, so it's making a long-
delayed debut in this memoir. In the ensuing 39 years, I've

either stifled or soft-focused some of my memories of the grittier aspects of life in Manhattan. Perhaps I've become mellower. Or maybe I've forgotten.

****

The other morning on West 113th Street, I came upon a cop about to ticket a lone car illegally parked on the north side of the street. On the south side, cars sat bumper-to-bumper in a double row along the entire block. Having observed this particular phenomenon before, I decided to inquire as to the legal procedures involved.

"Officer, how come you're giving him a ticket, and not bothering with all those double-parked cars?" I asked.

"It's after 11 and he's illegally parked," he replied. When I asked about the legality of the double-parking, the officer smiled and said something about there being no warning signs that referred to double-parking.

Further down the street a frantic, law-abiding citizen was attempting, hand on horn, to attract the owner of the double-parked car that was blocking his own. The owner hadn't shown up, but several people leaning out their windows were shouting obscenities at the hapless victim.

This type of irrationality ad absurdum is characteristic of what's going on in New York these days. Forget gracious living—the bottom has fallen out of any pretext of even nominal quality of neighborhood life.

Alternate side parking exists supposedly so the streets can be kept clean, but sweeper machines are a dying species on the Upper West Side of Manhattan. The streets are so filled with debris that urban archaeologists will soon be able to start sorting and dating according to the degree of decomposition.

Apropos of this particular subject, when is the last time you saw a pet owner cleaning up after a squatting dog? The pooper scooper seems to have gone the way of the ill-fated bicycle lanes—one of those grandly touted ideas prematurely flushed down the toilet after the hoopla died down and actual day-to-day implementation had to be considered.

On the other hand, who can really blame these pet walkers? What's one dog turd compared to the tons of garbage already festering on any city block? The "fouling" summons is as rare these days as that revised subway map so highly publicized a year ago.

The unavailability of the transit map is particularly unfortunate. Short of the dazed familiarity of borough natives, there is virtually no way most people can tell where they're going in this subterranean chamber of horrors. Inquiring of the token attendant is either asking for shouts of complaint from purchasers waiting in line behind you or a distorted answer blared out from a loudspeaker designed for Yankee Stadium. Most maps on platform walls or inside the trains have been defaced by graffiti vandals, called by some urban sociologists "the real artists of our time," law-breaking being an apparently accepted attribute of the not-so-creatively talented these days.

You may have recently experienced first-hand a new phenomenon beneath the streets of Manhattan, the presence of a subway vigilante group self-named the Guardian Angels, nifty in their lettered tee shirts, black pants, and red caps. My own impression of the Angels is that they resemble a group of ex-Green Berets with a change of hat color, stomping up and down train aisles, banging doors, and generally behaving as though they are onto something important that you and I haven't been sharp enough to figure out.

I can sympathize, however, with one woman I saw interviewed on TV who had just signed a pro-Angels petition being circulated by the Guardians themselves. "I don't even know what I'm signing," she said, "but maybe they can do something."

It's true that it would be nice to have someone besides the all-too-rare transit police admonishing those subway riders who see the stairways as convenient restrooms. On the other hand, to use the officially designated lavatories is to risk having your pockets emptied or to be the recipient of other kinds of unwanted attention, however "friendly" the latter may be.

So far there don't seem to be any platoons of Angels patrolling the streets. With the shameful, wholesale closing of government-funded hospitals, more troubled people than ever are evident, some of them cursing at one and all, others just sadly bewildered at their new-found autonomy. Panhandlers too are proliferating, often staring threateningly or heckling, somewhat vacantly, like bored movie extras who have played the same part over and over again. But you never really know if maybe this time they mean it.

Actual street muggings, on the other hand, have taken a novel turn. Not content with relieving their victims of cash and valuables, some thieves with a good eye now divest their prey of marketable attire. Sheepskin coats, Calvin Klein jeans, Adidas Gazelles, and ultra-suede dresses are current favorites.

What to do about this abysmal state of affairs? The answer certainly isn't going to be forthcoming from the present city administration. Have you observed how adroitly Mayor Koch deflects blame? Note his concerned, "I know, I know, it's terrible," and his use of pejoratives such as "dumb" and "stupid" when describing the newest street or subway outrage. We identify with the clever mayor and forget that perhaps he is closer to where the buck stops than we are and should not be behaving like a shocked and helpless visitor to the Big Apple.

In the meantime, if you venture out to visit a friend, you're going to feel like a doomed character in a cheap horror film every time you get into a self-service apartment elevator, especially if it heads down to the basement after you've pressed an upper floor button. Even if you're lucky and only a resident with an armful of clean sheets gets on, you yourself become the object of furtive stares. You don't know if it's better to make conversation ("Nice pattern on that percale...") or just shut up.

If I'm out late at night, I've begun walking down the middle of dark side streets instead of along the sidewalk. I'll take my chances with the occasional passing car or speeding cab rather than the sudden ambush of a would-be mugger hiding in the ground floor recess of an unlighted brownstone.

If you decide to go to the movies, be prepared to have smokers of various inclinations—Chesterfields, grass, the occasional cigar—light up all around you, no matter where you sit. And don't be surprised if several people carry on loud conversations, sometimes with each other, but often one-sided rants at the characters performing on screen. Ask them to desist at your own risk.

Wherever you go after dark, don't carry more cash than is absolutely necessary, wear old shoes, leave your newly purchased vintage French military coat at home, whistle a happy tune (unobtrusively), and hope for the best. But take heart: I haven't heard a super-speaker transistor radio bearing down on me in some time. Maybe it's just the cold weather. But hot time, summer in the city is just a few months away. Can't wait.

Always an Onlooker,
Never an Extra

Ratso Rizzo, scruffy and sour-faced, was facing me on Sixth Avenue and 56th Street. As he began to cross 56th, a yellow cab swerved in front of him. He banged on the hood, yelling "Hey, I'm walkin' here!," along with a few other choice remarks. Next to him, Joe Buck just took it all in, his sweet-goofy, gum-chewing visage never changing.

Real life? No. Reel life? Yes. This was one of several scenes from John Schlesinger's great 1969 movie *Midnight Cowboy*, filmed on location all over Manhattan. I guess I can say I was part of it, even though I was on the wrong side of the camera.

This particular segment has achieved urban legend status because of several versions of what really took place. Some say the cab episode was totally spontaneous. Others say no, that it was staged with an actor hired to play the cabbie. Over the years, Dustin Hoffman and Jon Voight, who played Ratso Rizzo and Joe Buck, his unlikely companion, have given conflicting stories.

I seem to remember that their walk and conversation took more than one take, and I think I recall Ratso banging on the cab multiple times. But it may be that my brain is simply replaying that sequence over and over again, one of many memorable moments in this cinematic tale of two lost souls on a downward spiral in the big city.

Other scenes in *Midnight Cowboy* were shot at the Lincoln Tunnel, in Greenwich Village, Midtown, and on the Upper East Side. I happened to be in Times Square one night a week or so later when, lo and behold, John Voight sprinted past me along the neon strip of then-porn theaters. For that scene, I do believe the camera was simply in a moving car—no set-ups, just nighttime shooting of the naïve and frightened Texas cowboy in flight.

A true movie fanatic, I never seemed to tire of watching the film-making process. Once, I was even lucky enough to observe the cameras in action—close-up and indoors—for several days. That was a real lesson in how films are made.

Before I decided that it was the academic life for me, I worked briefly in the late 1960s for a start-up advertising agency in midtown Manhattan. The CEO had a connection to one Sam Shaw, a photographer best known for his many shots of Marlon Brando and Marilyn Monroe, including Marilyn's famous blowing skirt image from *The Seven Year Itch*. He also produced films, including several by the director John Cassavetes.

One day we were told that Cassavetes' new movie, *Husbands*, would be shooting in our office. We didn't occupy a great deal of space, so we knew we were in not only for some disruption but also an opportunity to watch and perhaps mingle with famous actors doing their thing. Cassavetes, doubling as both director and actor, was one of them, and so were Peter Falk and Ben Gazzara.

It wasn't until I later saw the film that I really understood what the scenes filmed in our office were all about. Although Cassavetes was known to do extensive research and preparation for his films, he apparently also encouraged improvisation and on-the-spot dialogue changes.

In any event, for a week we watched as crews invaded our quarters, arranging complicated lighting, writing things down on pads, maneuvering microphones and cameras, and doing whatever it is that happens "on the set."

We, of course, were most interested in watching the actors. I believe Cassavetes was the only one of the actors involved in the scenes in our office, but Peter Falk and Ben Gazzara regularly showed up, as did Mr. Shaw.

What were they like? Cassavetes: charismatic, intense, focused; Gazzara: handsome, distant, seemingly oblivious to those of us watching from the sidelines; Falk: easygoing, with a killer smile and a kind word for everyone. Sam Shaw, I remember, seemed a gentleman and would stop to chat. Of course, none of us at the agency got any work done.

Our premises were hardly recognizable in the finished film, and the office sequence lasted all of five minutes. "Look, there's the hallway," I think I whispered to a colleague as we watched *Husbands* months later in some darkened theater. "And isn't that Michel's drawing board in the corner?" she asked. Of course, we were nowhere in sight on camera, but we were there all right, just beyond the out-of-range boom.

Fast forward a few years: During my time working at Columbia in the 1970s, I watched several film crews shooting in my neighborhood and on campus. In the decades since leaving New York, I've seen Morningside Heights pop up many times, most recently in the Spider-Man movies, and I always experience a moment of nostalgia when I recognize a familiar landmark. But it's not the same as when I was there, actually watching it happen.

Back in 1972, Barbra Streisand, then a big movie star and fresh from the enormous success of the screwball comedy *What's Up Doc?*, made a film called *Up the Sandbox*, a comedy-drama about a young and unhappy Columbia faculty wife and mother. There were several scenes shot on the Upper West Side, including one filmed a block away from my apartment building on Broadway and 113th Street.

I must have been on my lunch break from nearby Butler Library when I came upon the movie set. I hung around for a while, watching as the brief segment went through several takes—long enough for me to get a good look at Streisand and to appreciate both the care taken to trying to "get it right" and the tedious business of actually making that happen.

In this particular scene, the character played by Streisand is shown leaving her apartment building, a doorway entrance very familiar to me, and making her way around the corner to Broadway, baby in carriage and toddler in tow. She pauses at a flower shop and scoots in, leaving the kids momentarily outside the store. She emerges and they continue their walk up the busy thoroughfare.

Simple? Yes, in theory. But during the time I lingered on the periphery, they performed this routine several times, with much attention paid during the in-between waiting periods to the little girl toddler and the months-old, remarkably cheery baby in the carriage.

Barbra Streisand, more diminutive in person than she appears on screen, was involved in *Up the Sandbox* with her own production company. Though not the director, she was clearly very much invested in the process beyond her acting assignment. I and more than a few passersby gawked as she participated in focused and lively discussions between takes with the technicians and, I assume, the actual director. It was fun to watch her—then and later on, seeing the finished film—as both Barbra Streisand the superstar/producer and Margaret, the unhappy but ultimately hopeful wife she was portraying. I'm sure I left only reluctantly to return to my job in the hallowed halls of Butler Library.

A year or so later, also at Columbia, I saw George Carlin tape a segment of what became a syndicated TV special called *The Real George Carlin*. I'd been a fan of his and looked forward to watching the process. The first segment being recorded involved guests Kris Kristofferson and his then-wife, Rita Coolidge, and was taped on the big central quad just beyond the main gate, with the enormous domed administration building behind the performers and Butler Library with its glass and columned facade in the opposite background.

I don't recall the songs they sang, but there were many interruptions caused by glitches and/or more polished retakes of the performances. Kris, laid-back and in a...jovial mood, drank many cans of beer. Rita, quite beautiful, was restrained in expression. They didn't talk much between takes.

At some point, Carlin himself came out to chat with the audience. I never saw the finished show, so I don't know—or remember—if this was an "official" stand-up routine or if he was just improvising to help pass the time. What I do remember is that in the middle of some very funny remarks, he quite suddenly told an offensive faggot joke. This was so unexpected to me and the group I was with that we didn't quite know how to react. George Carlin? Mr. Liberal? The guy we all liked for his wit and irreverence towards the establishment?

After he finished, one of my more assertive friends managed to get close enough to tell him we were offended by what he'd said. He apologized, sort of, and indicated he'd meant no disrespect. But I never quite thought of him in the same way again, and that's what I really remember most about *The Real George Carlin.*

Several years later, not long before I left New York, a highly anticipated movie called *Cruising*, starring Al Pacino, was being filmed, mostly at night, all over the island. Directed by William Friedkin, who had achieved enormous success earlier in the 70s with *The French Connection* and *The Exorcist, Cruising* would prove to be his most controversial effort. Poorly reviewed and only marginally successful financially, the film has achieved a certain notoriety not only for its graphic depiction of a sleazy gay Manhattan subculture but also because of vigorous protests by the gay community.

I was not among the angry crowds on Christopher Street and at other Village venues such as the notorious Ramrod bar during filming at those locations, but I did witness demonstrations when shooting moved north to the Columbia/ Riverside Drive neighborhood. On a late, warm summer night, I watched as crews attempted to film a sequence on Claremont Avenue, one of the residential side streets near the campus. I say "attempted," because protesters shone bright lights down from the tops of buildings on both sides of the street, while others shouted and blasted music from the open windows of apartments.

It was a chaotic, unpleasant scene, all the more disturbing because of what we'd heard about the grisly serial murder theme of the film. I left without really knowing how successful the demonstrators were in stopping the shoot. Al Pacino didn't seem to be around that night.

I had mixed feelings at the time about these protests. On the one hand, I agreed that it was unfortunate that United Artists and Lorimar Productions had chosen to finance a film that could only perpetuate stereotypes that represented a minority of New York's gay population. Though the Stonewall demonstration had occurred a decade earlier, gay liberation still had a long way to go back then, especially as far as movie-going middle America was concerned. We didn't need this kind of ugly and sensational spotlight.

And yet...As Pacino himself explained in a later interview, the Mafia depicted in the *Godfather* films was certainly not meant to be representative of Italian-Americans. And I suppose the filmmakers had the legal right to focus on and film whatever story they wanted. Finally, I also knew from my own experiences that the skanky world depicted in the film was most certainly, for better or worse, a fact of life in 1970s Manhattan.

I haven't seen *Cruising* in decades. After I did view it in its initial release, though I didn't think it was meritorious as a film, I remember having the same ambivalent feelings I describe above. Were I to see it today, 35 years hence, I wonder if I'd simply consider it a curious and dated snapshot of the underbelly of a life that many of us at least sampled back in those days of early liberation.

From the sweaty back rooms of the Ramrod Bar to the elegant exterior of the Plaza Hotel is a huge leap in aesthetics and social mores, but another movie I witnessed in progress was *The Way We Were*, that 1973 blockbuster with Robert Redford and, again, Barbra Streisand. I happened by on the day a final scene from the film was being shot in front of that grand hotel, the Plaza, an iconic gem in the New York landscape.

In the plot, the two ill-matched, star-crossed characters meet again accidentally a long time after their inevitable split. Redford, looking handsome and elegant (and shorter than I expected) and hardly different from his younger patrician self at the beginning of the film, is entering the Plaza with his beautiful WASP wife. Streisand, older as well and now rather elegant herself in a fawn-colored wool coat, sports a trendy Afro, a tip-off, I suppose, that she's still out there on the front lines after all these years. In the scene, she is demonstrating with other "Ban the Bomb" protesters.

The segment in the eventual film consists mostly of close-ups of the two characters as they engage in awkward conversation, but the background, totally and very carefully staged, is impressive: strolling passerby extras doing their thing, noisy demonstrators shouting theirs, cars pulling up to the Plaza, the whole tableau alive with the cosmopolitan buzz of the city.

The entire southern half of Grand Army Plaza, facing the hotel and bordered by Fifth Avenue and Central Park South, was off limits to traffic and pedestrians. This was a big, expensive movie that obviously had received red-carpet treatment from the Mayor's Office of Film, Theatre, and Broadcasting.

Though I had only a glimpse of Streisand and Redford (there was some technical problem that delayed sustained action over and over again), that experience remains one of my best memories of watching reel life happen on the streets and avenues of Manhattan. And, unlike the other kind of life (the real kind), I can, with a quick flip of the switch on the DVD player, relive that moment, technologically restored and crystal clear, anytime I want.

Nights in Sheridan Square

T
he uprising outside the Stonewall Inn on Christopher Street in June 1969 forever changed the landscape of gay New York. Nearby Sheridan Square, then a grubby, paved traffic island at the intersection of Christopher and Seventh Avenue South, became synonymous with that momentous weekend riot.

But Greenwich Village had already been part of my life for several years before Stonewall. Though I never lived in that area of Manhattan, I spent a lot of time enjoying the pleasures that the Village, especially the West Village, had to offer. Long summer Saturday afternoons strolling around and browsing the bookstores often stretched into the early hours of Sunday morning on Christopher and other streets that led to the Hudson River.

Known since the mid-19th century as a center of the so-called bohemian life, the Village during the time I frequented it was the focal point for all kinds of counter-culture activities—in art, theater, music, and film. It's where the Beats and, later, the Hippies gathered, and it was the center of the gay liberation movement of the late Sixties, beginning, of course, with Stonewall.

I was drawn to Greenwich Village for all these reasons, but, cultural happenings aside, it was also simply a great place to meander on a lazy day. Many of the narrow and winding streets of the West Village are lined with elegant townhouses, tiny restaurants with varied and reasonable menus, and bars galore. The Village, where I headed virtually every weekend, was vibrant, exciting, and endlessly entertaining. Besides my Upper West Side neighborhood, it was where I most felt as if I were living the New York adventure.

Taking the clattering IRT downtown to the local Sheridan Square/Christopher Street stop, I'd often begin a Saturday stroll—occasionally alone, often with friends—by walking east on Christopher. We might stop off at Sutter's Bakery for coffee and a croissant, together costing less than a dollar, and then head over to the Eighth Street Bookshop, where we and several hundred other browsers would shuffle up and down the aisles of the always-crowded store.

Further east on Eighth, I enjoyed rambling in and around Washington Square, bordered by handsome brownstones from the days of Henry James but now teeming with young, long-haired families from the neighborhood; well-scrubbed and well-dressed teens from the boroughs and Long Island; and other kids from who-knows-where, some of them alone, disheveled, seemingly high, and reeking of the musty scent of patchouli.

Throughout the park, an incredible array of street performers provided a live soundtrack, musicians ranging from would-be Dylans to talented young men, mostly Caribbean Americans, beating out syncopated rhythms on blue steel drums. It was hard to decide what was the norm and what was incongruous: the staid and lovely townhouses on the periphery of the park, or the visual and aural cacophony of changing mid-20th century city life occurring within.

If I were out for the day with a friend, chances were good that we'd return to Sheridan Square for an early dinner at one of my two favorite restaurants in the Village, both now gone from the scene: Sweet Basil and Tortilla Flat. The former became known in the late 1970s as a premier jazz venue, but I remember it primarily for its glass-enclosed, plant-filled front and the crab-stuffed avocado and large pork chops offered on the menu.

Tortilla Flat, just south of the square, was where I ate most often on my sojourns to the Village. Its location, dimly-lit atmosphere, ethnicity, and incredibly cheap prices also made it my go-to place when friends or family visited for the weekend. Here's a sampling from a well-worn menu from the Sixties: tacos, rice, or refried beans, 30 cents each; a combination plate (taco, enchilada, rice, beans) for $1.15; and, at the high end of the menu, chicken mole, $1.50. And it was good.

After dinner, activities for the remainder of the night varied. It really depended on whom I was with, what had been planned, or what simply appealed on a sudden whim.

Taking in a live show was certainly an option. Long a center of experimental theater, Greenwich Village had also become, in essence, the new off-Broadway as skyrocketing real estate values forced many small, independent theaters to vacate Midtown.

Circle Repertory Company (Circle Rep), located on Seventh Avenue South midway between the Sheridan

Square subway stop and Tortilla Flat, was the theater I most often frequented. Founded in the late 1960s by an adventurous group of creative artists, including playwright Lanford Wilson, Circle Rep over the years garnered a slew of Tony awards, off-Broadway Obies, and a couple of Pulitzers. Up-and-coming actors I saw perform regularly included Christopher Reeve, Judd Hirsch, Kathy Bates, John Malkovich, and, especially, William Hurt.

I was dazzled by the Broadway shows I managed to see in my early days in Manhattan, but I think my passion for the theater really developed as I watched actors like Hurt perform on the small stage at Circle Rep. Before he went off to Hollywood and won an Oscar for *Kiss of the Spider Woman*, Hurt was a regular there, playing roles that ranged from a paraplegic Vietnam veteran in Lanford Wilson's *The Fifth of July* to the title role in *Hamlet*, and I saw them all. One night, as Lord Byron in a play called *Childe Byron*, he practically ended up in my lap after a particularly physical scene. You don't forget something like that.

If a play or movie had in fact followed dinner at Tortilla Flat, we'd sometimes then head over after the show to what became my favorite Village saloon, a tiny basement piano bar called Marie's Crisis, just off the Sheridan Square on Grove Street. The main attraction was an extraordinary singer/pianist named Marie (no relation) Blake, who had a huge following for many years. A woman of few words (though her occasional adlibs were spot on), Blake played a mean piano and offered an astonishing variety of tunes in her repertoire.

My favorite Marie Blake numbers and, apparently, hers too (she rarely failed to include them on any given night) were Cole Porter's sophisticated laments, "Down in the Depths of the Ninetieth Floor" and "Miss Otis Regrets," and a Calypso folk song from Granada made popular by Harry Belafonte called "Brown Skin Girl."

Blake played piano in a rhythmic, no-nonsense jazz style called "stride," an offshoot of ragtime. Fats Waller and Art Tatum were exemplars of the stride style. Marie Blake was a charismatic performer, so much so that when I learned she'd died in 1993, years after I'd last seen her perform, her songs played in my mind for days.

If the moon was full and the night was warm, I was occasionally tempted to top off an evening with a stroll down narrow Christopher Street, often described as the "Main Street" of gay New York. Several bars lined Christopher before it ended at the Hudson River docks. By the 1970s no longer in operation as working piers, the vast, deteriorating buildings offered a great deal of other kinds of activities for those willing to venture into their cavernous interiors.

However the evening or early morning hours ended, there was always a trek back to the IRT station and a noisy ride home to Morningside Heights. Before descending the grungy stairway to the train, I engaged in a ritual familiar to tens of thousands of New Yorkers: the buying of next day's Sunday newspaper, for me *The New York Times*, hot off the delivery truck and piled high at the street-level newsstand that never seemed to close.

Sheridan Square has seen some sprucing up in recent times. Some years after I moved to Connecticut, the paved triangle that formed the heart of the Square was excavated. In its place, residents and visitors now enjoy the Sheridan Square Viewing Garden. Not exactly gentrification, perhaps, but a beautification effort that would not have been forthcoming back in the 70s in that particular part of the Village.

In Christopher Park, another modest enclave a short block away, there has long stood a bronze statue of the Square's namesake, Philip Sheridan, Union military leader and later General of the United States Army. The ignominious observation that "the only good Indian is a dead Indian" is attributed to this stalwart hero of the Civil War.

At the opposite end of this pocket park, adjacent to the Stonewall Inn and not many yards from the General, stands sculptor George Segal's celebrated work, *Gay Liberation*. Consisting of two bronze-cast, life-sized couples, one lesbian, the other gay, the monument was installed in a celebratory ceremony on June 23, 1992. Times change.

Behind the Curtain: The Professional Children's School

I've just returned to Connecticut on Metro North from a late October Saturday in the city, where I had a rendezvous of sorts with a brief but memorable part of my New York past. I had the pleasure of seeing a former student, Karen Wyman, in her comeback appearance at the Metropolitan Room, a club in Chelsea showcasing talented performers in the city's thriving cabaret scene.

Do you recognize her name? If you watched the variety shows that dominated television 40 years ago—Ed Sullivan, Dean Martin, Glenn Campbell, Carol Burnett—you might have seen Karen, a teen-aged singer from the Bronx with an incredible voice—melodic, strong, controlled. Wyman was given a well-publicized buildup by Decca, which was, along with Columbia and RCA, one of the "big three" record labels. Had taste in popular music not been changing and had she not decided to raise a family in New Jersey, Karen's career would have taken off and stayed up there with the likes of Eydie Gorme, her idol, another kid from the Bronx with a powerful sound.

Karen was in my English class at the Professional Children's School (PCS), adjacent to Lincoln Center, where I taught briefly in the early 1970s. Not to be confused with the larger, public High School of Performing Arts (of *Fame* fame), PCS was nevertheless an exciting place to be, and I crossed paths with young performers from a wide variety of disciplines.

Founded in 1914 as a private school to accommodate the unconventional work and training schedules of young performers, PCS over the years encouraged and developed an increasingly eclectic student body. I taught Shakespeare, writing skills, and *Huckleberry Finn* to dance and music students, young actors (Amy Irving, Miles Chapin, Adam Arkin come to mind), champion ice skaters, and a few nonperforming children of professionals who often accompanied their parents on tour.

The largest bloc of students consisted of musicians and dancers. Like millions of other high-schoolers throughout the country, these kids would arrive at school early in the morning. But after a class period or two, dancers might leave for midday instruction—quite possibly by a former prima ballerina from Imperial Russia—at the School of American Ballet, the official training institute of Balanchine's New York City Ballet, just a few blocks away at Lincoln Center.

Musicians, too, would depart for nearby Juilliard for intensive lessons, perhaps on a string classical piece, from, say, a former first violinist or cellist with the New York Philharmonic. Then, back they'd come for afternoon classes, most likely to be followed later in the day by more practice off-site.

Some were really interested in their academic studies at PCS, others not so much. Some were as exceptionally bright studying English literature as they were talented in their chosen creative field, while other students struggled. But all (well...virtually all) shared one trait: They were disciplined. Even those not inspired by the challenges of literature and writing did what they had to do to get by. There was also a great deal of camaraderie and give-and-take among and between the students. I would guess that serious competitiveness, if that did exist, was probably reserved for the training classes back at the rehearsal studios.

A particular memory, somewhat melancholy, of the school remains especially strong. There was a day toward the end of each academic year when some exceptionally talented ballet students were selected for the company of the New York City Ballet. It was a joyous time for the chosen but heartbreaking for others who didn't make it. Often, these kids now had to scurry to improve mediocre academic grades for the probable alternative: four years of traditional college. Other ballet companies might beckon, but that initial rejection was perhaps an indication of the great uncertainties and vicissitudes of a competitive career in the arts. I always felt it was a harsh lesson to learn at such an early age.

Most of the time, however, it was great fun for me to hear backstage stories from the kids about what was happening in the ballet, concert and theater scenes in Manhattan. I also enjoyed overhearing conversations in the large commons room outside my classroom as students returned from practice sessions at their other schools. There was one ballet instructor in particular, a native of Russia and a former dancer with the Ballet Russe de Monte Carlo, whose exactitude engendered both fear and respect. I did get to see her teach a class at some point in the school year, and "Madame" scared me, too.

In later years, long after we'd all left PCS, I enjoyed following the careers of those who went on to fame and glory. A few dancers had long associations in Manhattan with the New York City Ballet, American Ballet Theatre, and the Dance Theatre of Harlem. Were they household names? Perhaps not, but anyone who followed what was happening in the world of ballet during the 70s and 80s would recognize the celebrity of dancers such as Fernando Bujones, Heather Watts, Daniel Duell, Stephanie Saland, Ronald Perry, and Marianna Tcherkassky, all of whom were in my English classes. Many others had substantial careers with other dance companies, and some are active today as master teachers or artistic directors of national and regional ballet companies or at high schools and colleges offering programs in the arts.

Ballet dancers, of course, begin their careers knowing that their time on stage is more limited than for most performers. As is true with athletes, time, physical stress and injuries take their toll, and most dancers begin to wind down by their early 40s. No one I taught back then is still dancing professionally today.

Some, like Daniel Duell, a principal dancer with the NYCB for many years, took their vision to another level. Dan founded Ballet Chicago, where the Balanchine legacy lives on. Another of my students, Victor Barbee, who went on to dance with ABT, became that company's Associate

Artistic Director. Achievements like these, from individuals significantly older now than I was then, make those years back at the Professional Children's School—vivid in my mind still—seem like a very long time ago.

It was a thrill, and remains a happy memory, to attend rehearsal classes as a PCS faculty member and to be invited to the annual gala, an event the School of American Ballet presented to showcase their very talented pupils. Seeing these kids on stage, in costume and executing difficult Balanchine dance steps and routines, usually with a poise and authority far beyond their years, was a far different experience from collecting their homework at the beginning of a 40-minute English class.

Unlike the dancers, my musician students didn't seem to face quite the same "rejection or acceptance" decisions so early in life. Many continued on to university, all the while juggling their ongoing music studies. I suppose my most illustrious student, a musician, was cellist Yo Yo Ma, a young man of exceptionally calm demeanor, as intelligent and nice as he was musically gifted. He graduated at 15 or 16 and went on to Harvard, as well as studying further at Juilliard and Columbia. When I see Yo Yo Ma perform now, occasionally in person and frequently on television, there is still something in his manner that harks back to the open-faced kid sitting attentively in my English classroom.

In addition to routine planning of their daily schedules, we also worked with children who needed to be absent from the school for longer periods of time. For example, when brother and sister Mark and Melissa Militano, national ice skating champions and Olympic contenders, were off competing somewhere, they studied via what we called "correspondence." I'd give them their lesson plans beforehand, and they'd send back their homework during their time away. It worked reasonably well and provided at least some continuity to their overall school experience.

In most ways, despite the heady atmosphere and the unusual teaching arrangements, daily life at PCS was similar to that at most schools. Parent-teacher events occurred regularly. I recall a lively chat with Adam Arkin's famous father, Alan, and his stepmother, actress and writer Barbara Dana, about our class reading list for that year. It was fun to remember that talk many years later in Amherst, Massachusetts with Barbara Dana, whom I've gotten to know because of our mutual love of Emily Dickinson.

Though I enjoyed my time at PCS, I was not settled in a career as a high school teacher. Nearing 30, I was increasingly unhappy about where my life was heading. I left teaching, pursued another graduate degree, and spent ten additional, very happy years in New York as a librarian at Columbia University. I continued to be a fervent (rabid?) devotee of the arts, and I never missed a chance to see one of my former students perform. From my Upper West Side neighborhood, that often meant just a long walk down Broadway or a short subway ride to Lincoln Center.

And that brings me back to Karen Wyman. I remembered Karen as a nice kid quietly occupying a chair in the back row of my English class. On the day she excitedly showed me a copy of her new LP record album, her photo prominently displayed on the jacket, I knew she was about to make it big.

And she did for a while. After our time at PCS, I followed her television career, bought her albums, and then lost touch.

A few months back, I happened to notice a blurb on "Broadway World," an online entertainment site I subscribe to, in which Karen's appearance at a prominent cabaret venue, the Metropolitan Room, was featured as an upcoming event. I bought a ticket and put the date on my calendar. She was great, and we reconnected at the club. Now, 44 years after those classroom days, we're friends on Facebook.

Thanks, Karen, for reminding me of a brief time in my life when I had the privilege and enjoyment of teaching a lot of talented kids off-stage. It's been even more rewarding watching some of them shine, over the years and even now, in the spotlight.

A Walk on the Wild Side

Whatever you've heard about the New York gay scene in the 70s could not approach what it was like to have been there. Depending on one's particular proclivities, it was exhilarating or demoralizing, trendy or squalid. It was Shangri-La or a queasy walk in the gutter. It was also the Garden of Eden with the snake about to strike.

Even at a remove of nearly 50 years, it's hard for me to sort out how I feel about that part of my life in Manhattan. On the one hand, it's become for me a grim symbol of the plague that was to descend by the beginning of the 80s. On the other, it's an experience I wouldn't have missed, though I'm sometimes amazed that I and thousands of others are still here, relatively unscathed, to tell the tale.

I say "relatively" because, of course, we didn't really escape the scourge. There are few people I knew at the time, and later, who were not affected, directly or indirectly, by the terrible toll that AIDS took. Many of us survived, many we loved did not.

I moved to New York in August 1963. In December of that year, *The New York Times* published a front-page article with the headline "Growth of Overt Homosexuality in City Provokes Wide Concern." As quoted in 1997 by Charles Kaiser in his compelling and highly readable book *The Gay Metropolis*, the piece went on to say "The city's most sensitive open secret—the presence of what is probably the greatest homosexual population in the world and its increasing openness—has become the subject of growing concern of psychiatrists, religious leaders and the police."

So there I was...according to the newspaper of record a participant in a great "sensitive open secret" and apparently someone viewed with "growing concern." I don't remember if I read that particular article at the time. I suppose that my behavior in those early years did reflect an awareness both of what was available to me as a gay man in New York and what I needed to do as a minority to protect myself.

Was I, as they termed it, "overt," a word as vague and unspecific as it is clinically blunt? Yes, in terms of having a perfectly happy social life at the bars and at dinners and parties almost exclusively populated by gay men. Not so much, I'd say, when it came to being comfortably out in my professional life, though if asked I would have been—and was—forthcoming.

And then came the Stonewall uprising in June 1969 and the beginnings of gay lib, followed by the 70s, a period in New York that has been described by photojournalist Allan Tannenbaum as "dirty, dangerous, and destitute." On the other hand, James Wolcott in a *New Yorker* piece wrote, "...

It's easy to over-accent the ugh factor and depict the 70s as a mammoth eyesore pothole out of which mankind somehow managed to climb...[nevertheless] it was not a decade for the dainty."

I'd second those remarks regarding what I recall of nighttime gay life in Manhattan, but I'd also add the words liberating, experimental, and yes, hedonistic. After decades of repression, gay citizens of New York were ready for action, both political and pleasure-seeking.

There were always many places for gay men to gather in Manhattan, even back in the days of police raids and strict regulation of so-called "deviant" public behavior. In my early years in the city—the mid-60s—it was easy and relatively safe to cruise outdoors on the Upper West Side on Riverside Drive or Central Park West, with an occasional detour into the Ramble, a 30-acre, densely wooded area planned originally as a "wild garden" by landscape architect Frederic Law Olmstead. Wild it was, more than Olmstead might have foreseen, and certainly dangerous later in the evening. It was not a place I frequented after dark, though many did, since it allowed for assignations without the need for conversation or an inconvenient schlep to someone's apartment.

On the fancier upper East Side, Third Avenue was the place to meander after dinner or a movie at one of the several Walter Reade art house cinemas that flourished at the time. Lots of young hustlers strolled along this avenue, and men from the suburbs cruised slowly northward on the one-way street, on the prowl for a quick encounter.

Occasionally I stopped at Harry's Back East, on Third in the 80s. Harry's had a long bar, at which the customers, mostly alone as I recall, sat or stood, drinks in hand. Unless I went with a friend, I always felt a bit uncomfortable as I tried to assume a disinterested demeanor and at the same time one open to a friendly hello, not the easiest mix of attitudes to project. You wore sweaters, slacks, and nice shoes to places like Harry's and a few of the other East Side bars. Further south on 56th off Fifth Avenue, the Candy Store, cattily described as the "Wrinkle Room," attracted an older clientele, and I seem to remember a jacket dress code there.

Greenwich Village was more casual, though the granddaddy of all the saloons, the venerable Julius' (on the premises since the Civil War) had an uptight, even schizophrenic, personality. Located on the corner of 10th Street and Waverly Place, Julius' was by far the best-known gay bar in Manhattan.

It wasn't until after Stonewall in 1969, however, that the owners and staff seemed to acknowledge its gay identity. Before that historic event, bartenders would tell standing customers to face the bar and not lounge near the long window that looked out on the street. That was legally termed "loitering." Three activists were denied service in 1966 when they declared themselves to be homosexual, a deliberate testing of civil rights that aided the gay liberation movement and gave Julius' a great deal of decidedly mixed publicity. I once saw Rudolf Nureyev at Julius', but that was a decade later.

Other favorite bars and night spots, not identified as gay per se, nevertheless had a strong gay clientele, places such as

Marie's Crisis, a basement bar over on Grove Street, where I swizzled many a Rob Roy listening to the fabulous Marie Blake belt it out on the piano. The Bon Soir, another small downstairs club on Eighth, regularly featured the legendary chanteuse Mabel Mercer. I missed Barbra Streisand, who got her start at the Bon Soir in 1960. Three years later, soon after I moved to New York, I did catch Streisand in her star-making turn on Broadway in *Funny Girl*.

The bathhouse was another feature of gay life in the big city. Though I was not a regular customer, occasionally I did visit the three most frequented: the Everhard, St. Mark's, and, later, the Continental Baths in the basement of the Ansonia high-rise, in its early 1900s heyday the most opulent residential hotel in Manhattan.

The Continental took gay baths to a new level of sophistication. In addition to a dance floor and a cabaret area, there was a waterfall that spilled into a small swimming pool, a restaurant, saunas, and, of course, small individual rooms for private entertaining.

Show biz entertainment became a drawing card at the Continental, a young Bette Midler getting her start at "the tubs," with Barry Manilow as her accompanist. Performers I saw at the Continental included singers Margaret Whiting, Melba Moore, and Larry Kert, the original Tony in *West Side Story*. The shows were so successful that it was not unusual for the audience to be composed of a sizable number of well-dressed, presumably heterosexual couples out on the town sitting alongside scores of gay men clad only in towels. You had to be there.

Later, the Continental morphed into Plato's Retreat, where lesbians and straight couples frolicked. When the male bathhouses were closed in 1985 because of the AIDS crisis, Plato's Retreat was initially allowed to stay in business. However, because it now violated a newly passed anti-discrimination law (!), it too pulled the plug shortly thereafter.

The Continental had opened in 1968, immediately preceding the Stonewall uprising (1969), which ushered in the 70s. There seemed to be not only a proliferation of bars but an upsurge and acceptance—or at least a tolerance—of extremes of nocturnal activity. Late-night goings-on, especially in parts of the Village, gave new meaning to a "Toto, I don't think we're in Kansas anymore" reaction that the big city has always provoked in some visitors.

The names of a few of the bars that flourished in those years give a graphic sense of what was promised, and mostly delivered, within: Ramrod, Ninth Circle, Anvil, Toilet, Boots and Saddle, Badlands, Eagle's Nest, Sewer, International Stud, and Mineshaft. Keller's, a leather bar where biker-garbed customers assumed intimidating poses, sold an S&M magazine called *Black and Blue* behind the bar. The Cock Ring, 'way over near the West Side Highway and the river, was situated on the ground floor of the not-so-elegant, pay-by-the-hour Hotel Christopher.

Nearby, there was always much activity in the deserted piers along the Hudson, as well as around and in the big empty trucks that loaded and unloaded freight from ships arriving at those nearby docks still in use. Streetlights were sparse in this area, and there was no light at all in the backs of the trucks, but the occasional flare of a match and the shadowy shuffling of scores of men outside and inside gave one a certain sense of place. Once I was surprised—but not as much as he was—to bump, literally, into a married minister acquaintance. I half expected him to tell me he was doing pastoral research, but he immediately fessed up, and we later became friends.

Occasionally, a siren would be heard, followed by the flashing red lights of a cruiser. I suspect the police were giving warning, rather than truly having, much less wanting, to deal with throngs of surprised men being confronted by headlights and flashlights. I don't recall ever seeing anyone actually arrested. After scattering in all directions, most men would return within the hour. There's a trucks sequence in a movie from the period called *The Detective*, with, of all people, Frank Sinatra, that captures to an extent the bizarre nature of the whole scene.

Unlike the nighttime-only activity at the trucks, cruising the deserted piers occurred 24/7. Weekend afternoons were an especially busy time. The huge, empty dock buildings jutting out into the Hudson in the meatpacking and Chelsea areas south of Midtown were in varying states of disrepair, ranging from broken windows and "open skylights" to floors in danger of collapse. But that didn't stop the traffic of men—young, old, well-dressed, half-naked, uptight, exhibitionistic—from traipsing through the dust, rubble, and general sleaze in search of personal adventure or a voyeuristic thrill. Both were readily and plentifully available.

Today, Pier 45, at the end of Christopher Street, has been cleaned up, rebuilt, and transformed into a park with green grass, young trees, and benches. There is even a stage performance area at the far end overlooking the Hudson.

As I strolled through the park on a recent visit, it was hard for me to imagine the look of the place 40 years ago. Many of the strollers were actually pushing strollers, and there was a family-friendly vibe to the place. I noticed a number of gay youth, a few of whom did have the look of kids with no other place to go. In the main, however, the scene was far different from the somewhat sinister though seductive labyrinth as I knew it.

Gone, too, are most of the local bars, including the notorious Toilet, Mineshaft, and Anvil. You entered the Toilet from an old freight-type elevator that opened directly onto the street. It was the kind of elevator that made you want to check the date of the last inspection, except that it was too dark to see anything. Inside the bar, clothes were optional, and leaving some of them in the "checkroom" was a good idea, depending on what activities you had in mind. The back rooms were dank and sticky, though there was a large dance area with a wooden floor near the entrance. And there were other rooms, where the kinky stuff occurred. In a tight group of sometimes 10 or 15 men, it was hard to tell who was doing what to whom. As far as other games, think of this bar's name and use your imagination.

The Mineshaft was of the same ilk, on an even more debauched level of activity. There were a lot of S&M goings-on, with participants acting out slave/master scenarios. Once or twice at the Toilet and Mineshaft were enough for me, though I can't deny the sordid allure of wandering through what seemed like a live, all-male, more explicit version of that Hieronymus Bosch painting.

Of all the rough bars, the Anvil, at 14th Street and Tenth Avenue, had the most glitz, at least on the main floor. There was continuous music and dancing, the smell of amyl nitrate ("poppers") permeating the air as customers inhaled to experience an extra rush. For me, the result was dizziness and slight nausea, so, as someone else once said, I never inhaled. Clearly, I was in the minority.

Naked go-go boys danced on a large circular bar or swung upside down from the ceiling, and drag performers paraded on another small stage. Other featured entertainers executed sexual gymnastics or feats of derring-do, such as dancing around and jumping naked through a ring of fire. Downstairs in the sub-basement was where customers created their own entertainment in a pitch-black, claustrophobic warren.

This is what I experienced of the New York gay landscape in the years preceding Stonewall and the decade that followed. After 1981, the year I moved to Connecticut, many of these clubs (in addition to the baths) were closed by the city. Although I've continued to go to New York frequently in the ensuing years, I have no idea what the current bar scene is.

Now, when I visit the Village, I still see the ghosts of those of us who were young and heedless, searching with newly achieved abandon for a momentary connection. Or, perhaps, in what W. H. Auden affirmed as our "normal hearts," in the hope of sometimes finding something more.

Falafels, Egg Creams, and Breakfast at Tom's

W hen Manhattan is your home, you don't so much inhabit the island as you do the neighborhood you're living in. It's hard for visitors, perhaps casually familiar with the neat grid of avenues and streets, to realize that within these seemingly identical geometric spaces are communities that function as little villages.

Thinking back on my years in New York, what I remember most vividly are my apartments and the surrounding shops and amenities that were the fabric of my daily life. Sure, I still miss the theater and the occasional fancy Midtown restaurant and the unparalleled museums, but I also long for familiar storefronts and open fruit stands and sidewalk book sales, usually within an easy stroll of my front door.

During my many years in New York, I called more than ten apartments home, all of them in Manhattan, except for a brief time in Brooklyn Heights. That particular borough neighborhood, with its leafy, flower-bedecked streets and lovingly maintained brownstones, was perhaps the prettiest place I lived, but its spectacular views of Manhattan only made me realize all too soon that I was missing being right in the thick of things.

I was a West Side New Yorker, and six of my apartments were on streets on or near upper Broadway, in Morningside Heights. The last of them was a spacious, rambling place in a big old building that took up most of the block between 113th and 114th Streets. I lived there for five years, far longer than anywhere else, leaving only when I moved to New England in 1981.

Built in 1909, Forrest Chambers, as my building was initially named and marketed, was originally a 12-story luxury building with apartments as large as ten rooms, all of them with maids' quarters and multiple bathrooms. Eventually acquired by Columbia University, the floor plans were broken up into smaller units leased to those of us "professional" staff who were lucky enough to win the approval of a formidable woman in the university's real estate office. This lady doled out "her" apartments in an imperious, noblesse oblige manner to a waiting list of deferential employees eager to get into one of those buildings.

Though its days of pre-World War I gentility were long gone, 601 West 113th Street maintained some trappings of its former self. After walking down a deep, canopied outdoor entranceway, you might have the door opened for you by one of the maroon-jacketed doormen on duty at all times. This amenity was as much a nod to neighborhood security as an indicator of luxury living; Columbia was a benevolent and protective landlord to those of us living in its "better" properties.

My apartment, four sunny rooms that you entered from a long, private hallway where I was able to hang at least 20 framed pictures, was on the eighth floor facing Broadway. A small Chemical Bank building had replaced a tall structure across the street, giving me an open-sky view and a generous glimpse of the towers of the Cathedral of St. John the Divine, one block to the east on Amsterdam Avenue.

I was indeed a lucky dweller, all the more so because of the virtually subsidized rent. When I left New York in 1981, I was paying $475 a month for this gem, not a tiny amount in those days but very reasonable even then for what it represented, and unbelievable compared to the Manhattan rents of today.

It's the neighborhood in the immediate vicinity of this particular apartment that has stayed so very clearly in my mind. With the relentless gentrification of the Upper West Side, much of what I remember is gone, but enough remains in this university enclave to remind me of the days when this was my little village in Manhattan.

Tom's Restaurant, on the opposite side of Broadway a block from my apartment, was a New York version of your typical diner, and the price was right. I often ate breakfast and lunch there alone, usually on the run, but when I went out to dinner with friends, the specials at Tom's couldn't be beat, especially the meatloaf with exceptional mashed potatoes and a vegetable du jour. The wait staff was no-nonsense but amiable. I especially remember Betty, a tall blonde who called me and everybody else "honey" as she raced around the restaurant, seeming to serve multiple booths of locals at the same time.

Years later, I was stunned one night when I caught an episode of *Seinfeld* and realized that an exterior shot of the friends' hangout featured Tom's red neon RESTAURANT sign. Inside, it didn't seem to be the same location, but for a moment I imagined myself in one of the comfy booths (the real Tom's were upholstered in red) enjoying a cup of pea soup, a BLT (hold the tomato), watching Betty balance impossible arrangements of platters on both her skinny arms.

Sometimes after lunch I'd stop off across the street at a storefront with a sign in Old World script letters that spelled "Mondel's Home-made Chocolates" above its awning. Inside the claustrophobically small space, glass display cases of candies—truffles, orange peel, almond bark, marzipan, turtles, buttercrunch—mingled their aromas with the chocolate that I imagined was bubbling in vats somewhere in the back reaches of the narrow store. I often wondered how there was space to concoct all these candy land goodies, but supposedly everything was made on site. Mondel's was especially popular during the gift-buying holidays, when lines would literally form outside the store all day.

I'd buy a few chunks of white chocolate and make them last the afternoon. In the winter, I might choose a few mousse balls instead—some milk chocolate, some dark—that in warmer weather melted too fast to last more than a few minutes, sometimes not long enough for me to make it back to my air-conditioned office in Butler Library, a few blocks away on the Columbia campus.

Although I usually like my sweets in moderation, I was also a pushover for a dessert at a local restaurant I frequented as much for its low prices and European atmosphere as the food, though that was appealing, too. This was the Green Tree, a Hungarian place over on Amsterdam Avenue, across from the massive Cathedral of St. John the Divine. The dessert I particularly craved was called palacsinta, a kind of crepe filled with jelly and topped, if you liked, with heavy cream.

The Green Tree offered other fare as well. I also enjoyed for starters the stuffed cabbage or the goulash, always accompanied by several kinds of vegetables and served to me and a motley assortment of local residents, many of Eastern European origin, by waiters with (I think) Hungarian accents.

For snacks and sandwiches, my two standbys were the Ta-Kome deli and a tiny Middle East joint, both within one block of where I lived and worked, and convenient for lunch runs or late- night food hankerings. The former was a typical deli/grocery, with packaged products arranged haphazardly along narrow aisles. The sandwich and deli counter ran along the rear wall, and throughout the lunch hour a long line, consisting mostly of Columbia students and staff, formed from the front of the store. I became friendly with one of the clerks, Carlos, whose sandwich-assembling abilities were second to none and who needed only to know whether I was ordering my usual roast beef, ham, or tuna before putting it together "with" exactly what he knew I liked.

I was introduced to Middle Eastern food, specifically the falafel, at what can only be described as a true "hole in the wall" shop on Broadway. This dark warren, was euphemistically named Prince's Sandwich Shop. Though you could squeeze inside (barely) to place your order, most of the time customers stood on the sidewalk and spoke to the owner/chef/cashier through an open window. I always ordered the same item: several deep-fried falafel balls (ground chick peas, onion, garlic, and assorted spices) on pita bread with lettuce and creamy tahini sauce.

During my years in that neighborhood, I spent a lot of coins on falafels, but considering they were only $1 a pop, that's eating cheap. And I've never had falafels since that measured up to Prince's. (For those who like really impressive statistics, the world's record for big balls was set in Amman, Jordan in 2012—a whopper falafel weighing in at 164 pounds.)

Despite the literally scores of eating establishments within walking distance, however, I did eat often at home. Grocery shopping for me in Manhattan was usually a several-times-a-week event. I never bothered to invest in a street shopping cart, so I had to haul whatever I bought several blocks back to my apartment.

I marketed on the corner of Broadway and 110th Street (officially, Cathedral Parkway) at one of the Daitch-Shopwell supermarkets that dotted the West Side. (In those days, Gristede's and D'Agostino were the other two big supermarket chains in the city, more upscale and generally located on the East Side).

Like the independent delis, large food chains were paying big bucks for their retail space, so the aisles were narrow, the shelves jammed, and the shopping carts less plentiful and smaller than the metal behemoths that you propel down the wide, polished aisles of today's suburban marts. Sometimes you had to wait for a cart to be emptied at the chaotic check-out lines, and even then you weren't sure of first dibs—not if an intrepid crone of indeterminate age, menacing scowl, and waving cane pushed ahead of you.

Old women (and men, though fewer) seemed to make up a sizable part of the population of my neighborhood. They were omnipresent on Broadway and the side streets, and I often wondered about their seemingly solitary lives as we passed. Perhaps that shopping cart behavior reflected what I imagined to be a bleak and mean situation—growing old and facing the end on a small income, all the while trying to survive the rigors of living in the big city.

A lot of older men did frequent the Mill Luncheonette, congregating for coffee and conversation around the smoke-filled, noisy center tables. Equipped with a soda fountain and cigar counter, the Mill also sold a wide variety of newspapers and magazines that ranged from *The Economist* to *Playboy* (and later, *Playgirl*)..

I liked the Mill for two reasons. They served a delicious egg cream, a concoction I'd never heard of until I moved to New York and whose ingredients were a mystery to me until I tried one at the counter. And, secondly, I was fascinated by one of the owners.

First, the egg cream: There is no egg or cream in a New York egg cream. The New York egg cream is made of milk, seltzer, and chocolate syrup. The origin of its name is unclear, with many possibilities suggested, including several having to do with the similarity of words in the names of other, similar drinks, e.g., *chocolat et crème*. A likely explanation is that egg and cream, relatively expensive, were dropped from what had been usual ingredients in 19th -century milkshakes.

I used to sit at the counter and watch one of the staff make my egg cream: A modest amount of milk was poured into a large glass, and a lot of pressurized seltzer was added and briskly stirred, creating a mound of bubbly fizz. A smallish dollop of chocolate syrup was then mixed into the concoction with a few slow turns of the spoon. *Voilà*: The New York egg cream.

Competing with the egg cream for my attention was one of the co-owners, who sometimes served, but did not make, my drink. He was of late middle-age, with sparse black hair and pale skin, and when he spoke, which wasn't often, it was with an Eastern European accent.

One day as he placed my order on the counter, I noticed for the first time a number tattooed on the inside of his forearm. I was stunned. Although I knew immediately what it signified, I'd never, to my knowledge, seen a concentration camp survivor. Later, I came to realize that I'd probably passed many on the streets of my Upper West Side neighborhood, a heavily Jewish-populated part of Manhattan.

From that day, I watched Morris—I believe that's what some of the regulars called him—as he went about his duties. He had a somewhat gruff manner and rarely smiled, and though he conversed with friends, we never exchanged more than the necessary words. His face remains in my memory as a reminder of the lives and experiences, unknown and unfathomable to us, of so many people we see day after day, especially on the streets of a big city neighborhood.

Besides Tom's Restaurant, perhaps the most famous neighborhood establishment I frequented was The West End, a bar located on the ground floor of what became my last apartment building. Over the years The West End has assumed legendary status as the hangout of members of the Beat Generation. Later it served as the site of so-called "back room" planning meetings of students involved in the 1968 campus uprising. But it's the ghosts of Allen Ginsberg and Jack Kerouac that gave the bar an aura of coolness, at least until it closed and re-opened under a different name in 2006.

Most of the time I spent at The West End occurred in the 1960s. I was certainly aware of the Ginsberg and Kerouac stories from the previous decade, which admittedly did lend a certain mystique to sitting in one of its well-worn booths, but it was basically just a convenient neighborhood bar. The Gold Rail, across the street a few blocks down, was the same kind of beer-and- hamburger or blue-plate special hangout, but it had a livelier, friendlier feel, and the food was better.

A decade later, when I moved into my last New York apartment, directly eight floors above The West End, I rarely patronized the bar, though it had a following because of the live music shows that played late into the night. Like most Manhattanites, I grew accustomed to the honking of cabs, the wailing of passing cruisers and fire engines, and other noises wafting up from below, including jazz combos and patrons departing in the early hours. It was part of the neighborhood scene, no more, no less.

It was only after I'd moved from New York and was well ensconced on the bucolic campus of the University of Connecticut that I realized the unique character of what I'd left. One day I was having lunch with a graduate student friend who was writing his English dissertation on the Kerouac and Ginsberg years at Columbia.

"You lived in the same building as The West End?" he asked in astonishment after I'd apparently mentioned something about my proximity to the campus.

"I did," I replied, "though it was years after they were there. I didn't know them, or anything like that."

Still, I felt a rush of, I guess, pride and then a wave of nostalgia as we continued to talk about those days on the Upper West Side. I was more than happy to oblige with my tales of the city.

Once a New Yorker...always...

Credits

"Dallas and New York: November 1963" first appeared in *Connecticut Authors and Publishers Association Writing Contest 2013-2014* (Amazon Digital Services).

"The Majestic Heart of a Campus" is adapted from an essay that appears on the Columbia University Alumni Website (www.columbia.edu/cu/alumni/connection).

"Taylor and Burton: with Liz 'n Dick in Times Square" first appeared in *Connecticut Authors and Publishers Writing Contest 2011-2012* (Amazon Digital Services).

"Up against the Wall! Part I: Columbia: 1968" first appeared in *From My Life: Travels and Adventures* (CreateSpace, an Amazon.com company), 2010.

"Where I Was when the Lights Went Out" first appeared in *Connecticut Authors and Publishers Association Writing Contest 2012-2013* (Amazon Digital Services).

"Up against the Wall! Part II: Stonewall: 1969" first appeared in *From My Life: Travels and Adventures* (CreateSpace, an Amazon.com company), 2010.

Photo Credits

Front cover: New York-based photographer Reynaldo Brigantty captures a Manhattan street scene familiar to anyone who has lived, worked, or walked in the big city. Coincidentally, the shot was taken on West 60th Street, and the façade of the Professional Children's School, featured in this book, is visible in the upper left corner. (#brigwork2; **https://1-reynaldo-brigantty.pixels.com**).

Back cover: This photo was taken by James Garnes, my nephew, in 2019 at the Iron Horse Music Hall in Northampton MA. The show was a tribute to James Taylor and Simon & Garfunkel, favorites of mine all the way back to my years in New York

Made in the USA
Lexington, KY
31 October 2019

56273162R00107